The
Diamond Cutter's
Daughter

The Diamond Cutter's Daughter

A Poet's Memoir

ELAINE TERRANOVA

RAGGED SKY PRESS

Princeton, New Jersey

For my family

Frontispiece: Elaine Terranova and her father.

Cover collage: Elaine in Europe, 1965, photo by Philip Terranova, and "Sansom Street, 1952," photographer, William S. Coward, *Philadelphia Evening Bulletin* Photograph Collection, SCRC 170, Temple University Libraries, Philadelphia, Pennsylvania. Photo page 129, "Leo Goldstein, Diamond Cutter," photographer, Frederick A. Meyer, *Philadelphia Evening Bulletin* Photograph Collection, SCRC 170, Temple University Libraries, Philadelphia, Pennsylvania.

Author photo, p. 181 and photo on page 176, "The shop on Sansom Street," by Olive Froman. Other photos appear courtesy of the author.

Lines from "The Diamond Cutters" in *The Diamond Cutters, and other poems* by Adrienne Cecile Rich, 1955.

This book is memoir. It reflects the author's present recollections of experiences over time. Some names and characteristics have been changed, some events have been compressed, and some dialogue has been recreated.

Published by Ragged Sky Press
270 Griggs Drive, Princeton, NJ 08540
www.raggedsky.com

Library of Congress Control Number: 2021931224
ISBN: 978-1-933974-41-5
Cover and book design: Ann Aspell
Printed in the United States of America
First Edition

However legendary,
The stone is still a stone,
Though it had once resisted
The weight of Africa,
The hammer-blows of time

—ADRIENNE RICH, "The Diamond Cutters"

CONTENTS

To name something, anything, is to choose it

The kitchen is where Mommy lives

My parents never go out without me

I want that moment to come again

The walls seem to have slid forward

TO NAME SOMETHING,
ANYTHING,
IS TO CHOOSE IT

Previous page: Cousin Esther and Aunt Lena.

My Name Is Esther

IT ISN'T, THOUGH IT WAS MEANT TO BE. ESTHER, THE FAIR-HAIRED girl, daughter of my uncle Sam, my mother's brother, her savior, she always said, for had he not brought her to this country? Otherwise, she would have perished with their siblings in a Nazi camp. She reverenced him as if he were a holy man. And indeed, the girl in the photo I'm looking at is fair, her blond hair cut at the nape in that blunt, '30s bob, so carefree, so stylish.

The framed photo sat on a little side table covered with a white lace doily in her parents' apartment. Aunt Lena has set a dish of Wilbur buds in front of it, I suppose for my sake. We are visiting the old couple in a big housing complex in the Bronx. My mother was invited and I came with.

It wasn't just the picture, a little faded and blurred with movement, as Esther stood in front of a pretty stone house with plantings. The small apartment her parents shared now was filled with the presence of the dead girl although she had never lived there, her spirit transferred with as much care as the rest of the furnishings. The place was dim and sad, despite the bright sun at the windows. But my aunt was friendly and remembered to say something to me every so often as I sat on a heavily upholstered chair, swinging my legs that didn't touch the floor and looking sullen.

"What a big girl you are now. I bet you're good in school." She asks what grade I'm in.

I answer shyly, then can't resist bragging. "I'm in the third grade but they're letting me skip 3B," which, I explained, is the second half.

She tells me with a smile. "You must be smart." Then she

3

turns back to the grown-up conversation. My uncle scarcely glances my way. His voice is harsh and he controls the talk, I can tell. He shouts and I think I see my mother cry, so that I know they are talking about the dead. If Esther had been the light of her parents' life, it seems she had been the light of my mother's as well.

I can feel how it hurt my uncle to look at me. Did he wonder why I should be alive while his darling was gone? I'm surprised to learn later that he's known in the family as a jovial man who has friends and a poker night, which my father didn't even have. A man who laughs, though now that would be hard to believe.

I'm staring out the window at the rest of the housing complex because that is the only thing for me to do. A new white building is visible across the way and it catches my attention. I see people in bathing suits stretched out on lounge chairs. Every once in a while someone gets up and jumps into a rectangle in the center, I imagine to quench their sunburn.

I can't actually see the turquoise water but I turn to my aunt. "There must be a swimming pool on top of that building," I say with excitement. "Can we go there, I mean after?" After the gloomy, boring talk was over.

"Later, dear, we'll go later," she says, smiling kindly, kindling hope despite my doubt. But the adults' conversation continues.

It is getting late and at last I understand this is where the afternoon will be spent. Ever after when I saw a rooftop pool, even a white building or a building the same shape, I thought of sun and swimming and denied wishes.

My mother believed a girl belonged in a kitchen, that reading would spoil your eyes and no man liked a woman who was smarter. Would she have understood Esther's ambition, her achievements, head of her high school debating team, A-student set for college, even a career? It was not a life she could believe in or envision for me. If she had known the real Esther, would she have approved of her? For when I wasn't satisfied with things as they were, such as no piano lessons, "Humpf, Queen Esther!" she'd throw at me, meant to keep me in my place.

My mother had long before put aside the idea of bearing another child. She had two, both boys, she had scored two times in a row. There was no reason to go through it again; she was a lady now. But then a few years after my cousin Esther died so tragically in that car accident—my uncle had pulled off the road to change a blown tire when someone plowed into them—there I was, floundering around in my mother's belly, finally "tearing her open," as she liked to describe it, and waiting for a name.

Though it was Esther she'd wanted, my cousin's name and our grandmother's before that, maybe my father didn't or feared it might jinx me. I was still "Baby Girl" on my birth certificate, never knowing it, until I was 16 and applied for a driver's permit. I might have guessed though since I was referred to simply as the Baby in our house, and on our street, generically, as "the diamond cutter's daughter." My childhood friend Kitty, in fact, long after we had both moved away and lost contact, remembered and found my father on Sansom Street, Jeweler's Row, where with her fiancé she picked out an engagement diamond to purchase from him.

I thought later my mother might have only been trying to protect me, to keep me a secret from the Evil Eye. Maybe I'd be safe if I stayed unknown to the world, that no bad things would happen to me. But to name something, anything, is a good thing, a way to choose it. You'd name a dog or a cat or a donkey you meant to keep. One name, maybe, but that would suffice. Once we had a cat with no name, it came to us out of the alley. We called it the Cat and it went away. We had a bird, a starling I found in the alley with a broken wing. My mother fed it milk-soaked bread till it was healed. It perched only on our shoulders, hers and mine, and flew around the downstairs and did its business mostly on a sheet of newspaper in the shed attached to the kitchen. For weeks we brought it to the park on one of our shoulders. There it hopped from branch to branch of the nearest tree and returned and we walked home with it again. One day, though, it flew up and up out of sight and didn't come back. It joined the other starlings in the wild. Oh, if only I had named it, I thought, so I could call it back. I went to the park on Saturdays and tried to coax one or another of the perching birds but none ever came. Surely, some magic resided in a name.

The actual Esther, the one of the picture, I was sure was inimical. I myself had mixed feelings toward her. I was sad never to have met her. We might have been friends. On the other hand, there just wasn't that much love to go around. Could I feel all that warm toward someone our mother cared for, maybe more than me? Would I want to be constantly reminded of her and what I lacked in the form of a name?

Jeweler's Row

Found: the little brown leather memorandum book my father dropped, edges foxed and feathered with use. Gray pencil soots the pages like a shadow of his own demise. Names and columns of numbers have been captured here in their prison of lines, where he borrows from the future, puts done to the past. And all of it flattens to a rubber band in his jacket pocket. Messages to himself, reminding what is owed him by the world.

SANSOM STREET. ONLY A TOURIST WILL PRONOUNCE IT RIGHT; native Philadelphians say Samson, like the strongman in the Bible. It was Sansom's Row in 1799, named for its developer, William Sansom, the first unified block in a city of row houses. In time, it became home to engravers and jewelers and then the first diamond district in America.

In the 1950s, when I knew it best, runners dashed out without coats even in winter to do an errand, make a delivery. Jewelers kept the transactions in their heads, on trust, only a note in a little book like the one my father carried to back up the sale. I see hesitant young couples, peering into display windows at engagement rings. They want to buy wholesale, hope for a bargain. Mingling among them, rich older men with women in furs on their arm, for whom a diamond purchase is not such a rarity. Also, New York dealers down from 47th Street one day a week, Wednesdays, as I recall. Hasids in black suits, their long side curls spilling from wide black hats, bringing with them packets of diamonds, "the rough," from the international trade, for my father and other cutters and merchants. My father will open and pore over these parcels in his little shop. What he seeks above all, the perfect stone.

Soon, it's said, pile drivers will be pushing down into the old soil, razing the first four buildings on Sansom Street's south side in order to erect a 23-story condominium tower. What will happen to the jewelers still in business here? Or, as a *New York Times* reporter pointed out, to the love stories of couples over the years who came for rings to seal their vows? My father's shop was on the same side, farther up, on the third story, not at eye level, so you wouldn't notice it from the street if you were passing.

A sign was stenciled over the two half-windows that stretched across the narrow property. It could have said JEWELER, capitalized in gilded letters like other, larger plate glass windows at street level, meant to attract customers. But more specific, more modest, in cap and lower case, black with narrow serifs, it read instead, Diamond Cutter, and above that, N. Goldstein, my father's name. Later "and Son" was added when Leo came to work there, that appendage not removed and still not revealed after he became a full partner. Even when my father retired and Leo had his own son with him as a setter, it was still nominally my father's business.

There was no showroom, the shop open just to the trade, not retail, and scarcely anyone else even knew it existed. The only furnishings, two high stools set before the benches my father and brother sat at in their gray coveralls to cut, a couple of cabinets, a set of delicate, medieval-looking scales, a chair where a seller or buyer could park himself for a transaction. Greasy dust settled over everything, diamond dust, blackened by oil used to prompt the wheezing, turning wheels where the stones were ground to shape. The whole room vibrated with the buzz.

A small aisle separated my brother and father, just wide enough for passage. A sink in the corner on my father's side, used for cleaning up and in an emergency, when my father was old and sick, that he could pee in if he couldn't make it to the bathroom down the hall or if he felt he was being followed or spied on and became afraid to go out. I remember the heavy pebbled glass door, usually kept open while they were working. An iron chain-link gate, black and fuzzy with grit, lay just before it and shut the little room off from the rest of the dark third floor. A buzzer at my father's right allowed passage to those who were expected. The gate might stop a man running in to steal the goods, how they refer to the rough and cut diamonds, but the latticed iron gate wouldn't stop a bullet.

Rough

MY FATHER IS ROUGH BUT VERY FORMAL. HE BATHES TWICE A day and wears a fedora, carefully pinched. He lifts it to ladies he passes to say hello. He dresses in a three-piece suit he wears from the house to work, gray or brown, which he changes for his mechanic's coverall to sit at the bench and grind the rough, ugly stones that look like rock candy but that will turn and shine, chafed into diamonds. One circles on the wheel, a pumice about a foot in diameter, like a phonograph with arm and needle, only the needle is one point of the stone. He holds a hand to the clamped diamond to steady it as it passes with its little whine and the other hand to raise a jeweler's loupe to his right eye. He makes jokes and he laughs because this is his work, and also what he likes to do. Sometimes he disengages a hand to pour oil onto the rotating lathe so that it is not unnecessarily abrasive. Rough to smooth, that is my father's labor, that is my father.

After the first heart attack I go to the hospital and find a lotion that nurses use to massage his feet. I rub away calluses, roughness. It is a kind of anointing. My hands move, pressing gently, deeply into the fat pads of his feet and up to the shiny scars that lace his ruined knee. It is strangely like stroking my own feet. I find things to say from long ago and he has to think to answer but does despite the effort, even if he doesn't normally trust words. Many things he says are sweet and loving, meant just for me. What else is there for him to do beside read the paper and wait for the nurses? But there's more to it. I feel I am massaging his heart. Though I am married now, though I belong home with someone else.

Animal

It's true there is sadness but pleasure too, in remembering. That is what I often do in the cabin in the woods on weekends. I am older now than my father ever was. I sit at the screened glass doors, smelling the passage of night animals in the woods, bitter smell but piquant, full, like the dark. Something knocks on the wood of the house, four paws, I don't know what. I'm listening to *Boris Godunov*, the melting duet of tenor and baritone. Then the grasshoppers begin their jagged etchings on the night. The monk and the blind man. Boris sings and dies a martyr's death. Maybe it's a skunk I smell or only a raccoon. Animal close but unknowable, something I can't see, but which probably sees me. Passing the leaves of a bush, taking a breath. I can't place that slow rasp. Uncertainty or hesitation. The way an animal is all choppy movement trying to gauge what's safe. Or the long, living death, something like a calculated sleep. I've seen squirrels and deer do it. Once a road-hit groundhog, pretending to die before it died. There was nothing to it, some instinct. Could we do it too? It broke my heart to watch.

I move to the banquette below the wall phone and everything changes. That grasshopper chorus reminding me of the strength of the insect population. That every square of the grid of the world is plugged. Meanwhile, the treat of picking up a book, some history or biography, and breaking it to the middle where there are pictures.

Loved Ones

HOW I STUDIED THEM, MY FAMILY. AS IF I COULD LEARN A LESSON in life just by looking. In truth, there were two families in my family. I was the second, unexpected, like the second brood of a summer. The first was my two much older brothers, desired, planned for. One, almost a man, was amused by me, benevolent. To the other I must have seemed a rival. I took his place, albeit 10 years later, at our mother's breast. He liked to tease and make fun of me, nursing so long, so long I can almost remember it. Two brothers, Leo and Sidney. I ran to both, though one I sometimes ran from. It was Leo, the oldest, who invented the fruit-crate scooter that Sidney sat me on before him and used to zip us down Franklin Street on sparking skate wheels. I learned to dance with my shoes off standing on Leo's cordovan wingtips. When he and my father came home from work, I jumped into his arms, or my father's, whoever was first.

Once I didn't even bother to open the door and, in my eagerness, smashed through glass. My mother wrapped me in kitchen towels and Leo ran before her, carrying me to the trolley we would take to the pediatrician's for stitches, Dr. Pearl, a pearl of a man, she said, but who like my mother was getting too old for this. Kitchen towels, of course, were first aid of choice. My mother often recalled Mrs. Lansky, the lady across the street where the lawns were higher. It was winter and the steps "were like glass." She wasn't holding onto the stovepipe railing ("See?") so she fell and "split her head open." They came then with kitchen towels but could do nothing. It was too late.

Leo, the loved one, "Lovela," as I heard my mother refer to him and I did too, though maybe she was saying Levela, for

Lev, his Jewish name. He was her firstborn, not necessarily her favorite. He and I both ran away from home at an early age. Leo, at three, apparently when Sidney was born. I, maybe in imitation, at five or six, from our new house where Sidney was left to "mind" me, which I knew he did, a lot. Hadn't I stolen from him my mother's attention if not her heart? Sidney. Sheila she called him, a girl's name, I thought. Much later, I found Shelag in the Bible, Judah's younger son, and that made more sense.

And who was that pinching my toes, "One little piggy, two little piggies," creeping up my leg. Oh, and *flutter under the bedclothes... playing "tent"... peek-a-boo!* He could be my best friend, laughing and playing, but unpredictable, turning on me in a minute. I remember the interesting and peculiar torture he had invented that day I ran away, the slow drip of grape juice down the neck of my pajama shirt.

My mother would only say, "Your Sheila (Shelag) loves you," when I told on him. It may have been away from home but it was toward my mother that I ran. She was still walking the mile and a half to Mr. Krantz, the irascible kosher butcher in our old neighborhood, a red-faced giant in a blood-spattered apron. I'd jump as he smashed his cleaver down on the chopping block and cling to my mother's skirt.

Miraculously, as in a dream, I followed along the crooked fairy-tale street with all the garages. Somehow I was able to find the butcher shop, but my mother had already left for the fishmonger's or the baker's, everything you'd need lumped together in the old neighborhood, like a *shtetl*. The butcher's kind wife, who stood patiently at the counter with her swollen legs, thought of me as lost, a little lost girl. But I wasn't. I knew where I was and where I was going, to my mother who could make everything right if only she would. Who made wonderful pies and had a cake with white icing to celebrate my birthday. That mother. Only she wasn't there, which made me feel alone and lost for the first time. The butcher's wife tried to keep me with her until my mother could return. But I wanted the safety of our house. Surely, my mother would find her way home where she belonged. I hightailed it back, fearing I would get a smacking whether she caught me then or later.

I remember my mother beating down on my shoulders as if to nail me into the ground. You'd think she'd just be happy to have me back. But even Sidney was sometimes sacrificed to the gods of rage. I notice later how he and I have the same physical trait, hunched up shoulders, as if warding off blows. She got him that day too.

My father, though, hit me only once. I was little, it was before I ever went to school. We were on a bus. Always motion sick, I was preparing to throw up, probably screaming in a pretty high register. Someone as self-conscious as my father couldn't bear it, the eyes he imagined focused on us because of his limp or my mother's loud voice. He came back from where he had gone ahead to silence me with a slap. I was so stunned the screeching stopped, and too scared to throw up. After that and maybe out of shame he avoided me for years. But came back to me, once, once. I was 16 and fell headlong down the shiny wood staircase, and he came to rescue me. "Dolly," he cooed, "Dolly," lifting me up. A parenthesis to the infant fall down the cellar steps when he destroyed the little rocker he had bought for me on which I accidentally somersaulted down.

Sometimes even Leo hit me. I suppose I was a pest, but he never had to mind me as Sidney did because he was always off with his friends playing ball or, when he was older, at work for my father. Still, we had quality time together and he taught me to curse and dance, particularly splits and shuffle steps from movies. My favorite thing Leo did was to come downstairs in the morning singing to the tune of "O Sole Mio," "O sole mio, my name is Leo."

The Race. The Fight.

THE RACE. THE FIGHT. IN OUR HOUSE, THESE WERE SACRED
words. There might have been only one of each, in eternal rota-
tion. During the race, my father would be egging the TV on, as
if it itself were doing the running, not the tiny spider animals,
crossing left to right. And my two brothers beside him on the
red mohair couch, too, bawled out encouragement and insults.
They were glad to be beside him, father, in the same awake, alive
state without the curtain of the newspaper drawn around him.
"Curly," they called him, though there wasn't a curl or anything
else on his head, or sometimes, "Old Man." But the effort it took,
this lame, heavy man, to get back each workday to the tasseled
lamp and easy chair. So what if I wanted to watch something
else. So what if I jumped at the banging of screen doors all down
the block when the men came in to watch the race in their hous-
es. I still see the grid of sunlight our door made on the straw
summer rug. The haze of voices and light. The wives not daring
to leave hot kitchens until the race was run, the bugler bugled,
the announcer became hoarse, the men dispersed.

One thing compared, only one. The Friday Night Fight.
Gillette razor blades marching to their theme song. The gong
and black blood speckling gray faces. Near-nude men dancing,
holding one another up. "Lookit that jab!" My dad again making
a confederate of the TV, as if my brothers were not there. Some-
times he went to the arena though and took my brothers with.
I begged him to let me go. But he wouldn't, ashamed maybe
that he loved it so, to see the two men who scarcely knew one
another punch away until one fell. How could he take his own
little daughter to a savage place to watch people bleed and fall—

blows bouncing off the sweet spot of someone's skull? Smiling, he told of managing fighters himself in the '20s when he was a brash young man looking to make a buck. And he pointed to the referee, was he really our relative, Ruby? Daddy said so and loved it, that blood connection.

Gypsies

ON SUNDAYS, ONE AUTUMN, MY PARENTS TOOK ME TO THE GYP-sies. They lived in storefronts on South Street, behind glass like goldfish. They cooked and ate and slept there. We stood outside looking in. Sometimes a boy waved or a man made a menacing gesture and turned his back. Once a lady in a shiny satin dress came out and took my hand. She told my future: a red-haired man and money. My father pulled me away in case they'd try to steal me. My mother, though, had known them from childhood. In Hungary, her father had driven her in a horse cart from the *shtetl* to the town, past their campfires, watching them dance. At Halloween she dressed me in a white blouse and her own skirt. She wound three flowered kerchiefs over my head and my shoulders and around my waist and made me into a gypsy. Over it all, I put on the heavy wood beads I had strung from a kit. When we next went to South Street though, we couldn't find them. They were gone as if overnight, leaving only dust and emptiness like a departing army.

Fireflies

I AM BESIDE A LAMPPOST AND A CONE OF LIGHT FALLS LIKE DUST over me. It is a late summer evening, hot and sticky, but I like how I feel, moist skin cooling. The fathers have come home, climbed up the steps that cut through high lawns to the white frame houses, and I am allowed out for a little after dinner. I hold something in my cupped hand and make a little opening between my thumb and index finger. Even away from the lamppost, I can see the glow. Sidney has given me a jar with holes in it and grass on the bottom. I rush inside to find it and put the thing in. I set it on a windowsill and watch a code of off-and-on beams, a message I can't understand. It beats against the glass. What I want is the light though. That's what makes it different from other bugs. If I take it out, I can keep it to look at by itself. The light is beautiful, I think, but not the bug. And I do and Leo comes over. I can tell he is a little horrified. "You killed that insect. It was alive and you killed it. Is that what you want?" But I want the light. I want it to be mine, to belong to me. Then I wouldn't have to be scared of the dark. I look at the fluttering thing in the jar, the tiny bright ball on the windowsill, getting dimmer.

Traveling Carousel

IS IT TRULY A CALLIOPE PLAYING "CRUISING DOWN THE RIVER ON a Sunday Afternoon"? I don't know that the music is recorded and the animals themselves are not making a sound. It is magic. I am so excited—a merry-go-round and it is stopping right in front of us on Franklin Street! The mechanism is welded to the bed of a pickup truck and the burly driver wears a straw hat and has hairy arms and big muscles. All of it reeks of grease and gasoline but I don't care. I run down the steps from the porch as I hear the first notes and eagerly wait while it backs into the empty space before my house. The odd vehicle. The valiant creatures in their garish varnish.

I have shinned myself on the metal frame of our beat-up porch glider getting off so fast, looking up and down the street for what feels forever. I see a horse and a goose and a camel, a lion and tiger I don't like to think about. "Mommy," I yell, "give me money!" It's a dime and the driver helps my mother load me onto my first choice, the camel, safe between its two humps. I am the only passenger for this ride, before the other children from up and down the street see and come running. Why do I want so desperately to spin around until I'm out of my senses, as when I turn and turn in circles to make myself dizzy?

Magic, magic, magic! The song blasted out to the street through a loud speaker. Me, saddled so I don't fall out of the truck bed. Dizzy with blue sky and sun and puffy clouds in their own shapes of animals.

The orange camel leers as I mount him and I throw my hands around his long neck. His skin is not soft as I imagine, like Teddy or the baby chicks I pet at Easter in the 5 & Dime, but hard to the touch and shiny-smooth. His expression is fixed, and he doesn't turn around to look at me. He is only a machine on a pole that travels up and down and around. He will never know me.

Time is important. The animals are only my associates of the moment, no grass nor sandy ground where they will loiter to feed, only the circular click, click of the track they know so well and can't escape. In this, I am a part of them, I alone, alive. The lion and the tiger are relentless in pursuit. I would not admit to being alarmed. But maybe they are catching up? Up and down and around. The man is hunched over the switch, making it all go. This may not be fun for him. I wonder he doesn't smile.

The ride goes on and on, the way every day careens into the next with no warning, but too soon it lurches and stops, over, what seems, before it began.

Tantrum

THINGS ARE VERY HARD IN THE WORLD OF A THREE-YEAR-OLD. So much you are born not understanding. You can play in the street but only until supper. You get a *potch* (smack on the behind) for the interesting white balloons the size of sausages you find discarded there and try to blow up. You can't pee in a bottle like next-door Bobby, so must hurry home or wet yourself. After supper night comes but not always sleep. You are safe while there is light. Then the light gets put out.

Now that you are three, no one touches you. You are too big suddenly for anyone's lap or to be slung sideways over a hip. Sometimes you say your back itches, "Please scratch me." But more than likely you will be told, "Rub it against the door frame. That will work." You will never be kissed now. But you must be loved. Don't they boil the water they give you when you are sick or because there's polio, to keep you safe?

And there would have been kissing sometime, even if you don't remember. For instance, while she was feeding you like a baby bird. No, passing the chewed peanuts, mouth to mouth, Mommy to you. Until it is a liquid froth you can swallow.

It's afternoon, and for some reason you are inside, not out in the street, running or playing hide-and-seek behind trees or going under the hose a neighbor mother holds, as you usually spend your days in summer. Maybe she has forbidden you: "Do you want to get polio?" Both of you are here in the small front room off the porch. There is only a chair, maybe two, a straw rug. There are no pictures, not even photographs, on any wall. Your mother sits, unmoved, unmoving. She is looking straight ahead as if in a trance, as if she doesn't see you although light from the wall of windows falls over you where you lie, face down on the floor. She is in her slippers, as always in the house. Her hands rest on her knees above the rolled-down nylon stockings. You are crying harder than you ever cried. You can feel your face getting red as you rhythmically bang, bang your sticky, throbbing head against the floor before her.

Fan

WHEN WE WANTED MECHANICAL THINGS, APPLIANCES, FOR IN-
stance, we went to the Sears on the boulevard. It took three buses
to get there, then a walk across the dangerous many-laned Roo-
sevelt Boulevard, more like a highway. You could buy clothes
there but not very nice. Once, years later, my mother bought
me black jeans. Jeans were just becoming a style, maybe from
western movies, and the popular girls all wore them so I wanted
some. But these jeans left a black imprint on my thighs and my
mother blamed me for insisting and for the return trip that was
needed to bring them back. But at the time I am speaking of, I
wasn't even with my parents when they went. I'd have been too
little, and they took the long trip without me to the grass-lawned
red brick building with so many windows and came home with
a big box. It was summer and the weather was predictably hot
and sticky, it was Philadelphia, after all. My mother told me that
in the house in the Bronx where they used to live before I was
born, they, my brothers, and all the neighbors sometimes slept
out on the roofs when it was hot at night, though it was never as
hot there as here—what bothers you most is "not the heat" after
all, "but the humidity."

"Did everyone wear pajamas," I asked? "Of course they did,"
said my mother. I only wondered if they slept fully dressed as
you would when you went out of your house on the street, for
instance. Soon the box was opened and a large fan taken out.
It sat on the table that went across the front wall where there
were windows and good light, in my parents' bedroom. Where
Sidney did his homework. Even later, when I had homework, I
wasn't allowed to use that table but did mine on the oil clothed

kitchen table. They took the wrappings off the fan and plugged it in. A wind started up with a great noise and blew the cloth on the dresser partly off until it was anchored at both sides with a hairbrush and a jar of hand cream. I walked back and forth in front of it and felt the breeze.

My parents talked about putting a bowl of water and ice cubes in front of the fan to make the room even cooler. I watched for a long time. The fan itself never jumped around but sat where it was put. It watched me and turned and watched me from a different vantage point, so fast I didn't see it move. What was making the whirring or blowing the air into the room? Even inside the fan's cage nothing seemed to be happening. It was necessary to investigate further. Something might not be right. Maybe Mommy and Daddy had been tricked. So I picked up the ruler conveniently left by Sidney next to a pile of books on the table. I'm sure I hesitated before I did it, but then daringly I stuck the ruler through the wire fence where the blades should be turning, which made an enormous noise, as it happened, its last. The sound of the fan and the wind, both, all at once stopped. So then everyone came running and I saw that the fan had been working—just too fast for me to see—because now it wasn't, it was still.

Like a Russian Winter

I REMEMBER MY MOTHER IN ONE OF HER BLACK DRESSES, PINK body drawn tightly beneath it into her corset that laced like a shoe. She had a wardrobe of black dresses she wore only for dress up, to go out of the house. Maybe not that time, though. If the street was solid ice all the way, how would she get to the hospital? No, I think I was all alone in the cold white room with the proctologist, Mr. Krantz's nephew. All our medical specialists seemed to be related to the butcher. His nephews were brilliant but equally gruff, doctors of every stripe, dentists. So I faced by myself this angry man, and how I got there, across the frozen trolley tracks and past the hospital victory garden of snow-smothered, withered vegetables grown to feed patients, was quite mysterious, like a folk tale.

Why should come first. I was seven or eight. I had been in bed with my customary winter bronchitis. My mother chugged up the coal furnace and brought me pastel lollipops that looked like pompoms. I was scarcely awake, scarcely moving in the upstairs dark, waiting for my father to come home when he sat a few minutes with me before he went into the bathroom to wash up for supper. He spent so much time in there, and with five of us, it seemed always to be occupied. O.K. So *why* was because I hadn't gone to the bathroom for over a week. Every day my mother would bring me up breakfast and say, "Well?" And every day I had to disappoint her. I ate and drank, steaming foods that came upstairs from the kitchen on a flowered tin tray, mostly cereal or soups and hot lemonade: tea with honey and citrus fruit, often a shot of whiskey to loosen my throat and the rest of me.

It was decided that the butcher's nephew see me, but we are

back to *how*. I couldn't walk on the ice, any more than my mother could in her Cuban-heeled orthopedic shoes. That's where my brothers were called in. Down the wooden stairway and out the front door, then over ten slick stone steps, I was carried into dazzling day. I was very fat, like a fat princess, and they seated me in the middle of the varnished wood—of my Fearless Flyer sled!—and told me to hold on. Two ropes were threaded through the front of the wrought iron frame, one for each brother to pull, like horses. A green-eyed horse and a black-eyed one. Did I only imagine the snowball fights that stopped the progress of this strange procession across the trolley tracks and up the drive and the sloping hills of the hospital grounds? The tinkling of sleigh bells carried off on the wind and distant, fearsome howling of wolves?

Summering

New Jersey was the other side of the Delaware River, the other side of our lives. Atlantic City, where we were headed. It wasn't really a city, only a strip of sand shored up against the Atlantic and a sugaring of sidewalks and stoops with fine, white sand. The whole state had spent much of its life under the ocean. Along the roads, stands sold tomatoes and fruit all summer because the soil was rich for growing.

I was sure it was always summer there and that's where I did my growing. We boarded the ferry, mother, father, brothers, I, passage to another world. A bootblack stropped with his cloth my father's high, crippled shoe, finding a rhythm, back and forth. The grown-ups quarreled and complained. Do you have the lunch, do you have your hat, do you have to go to the bathroom? We tugged shopping bags and straw suitcases in our wake. Then, like a musical command, fast but not too much, we breached the water and came to Camden where we paid again and climbed up to the waiting railway carriage. It took off with its fat head of steam, wobbling on skinny steel tracks. No one to wave or see us off, all accounted for, a family, a set.

At the guest house, we had kitchen privileges. Because of the damp, bread from the breadbox was blue where you cut it. A Spanish family gave me orzo and hot sauce to try. The father, for fun, colored photographs that brought dead faces to life. The air smelled of salt. My skin tasted salty when I licked my hand. The landlady's twins, Gert and Flo, were middle-aged and didn't look alike. Sometimes they combed their mother's wavy gray hair while she sat with closed eyes, spread and stolid as the sea. Sometimes they washed the porch and I had to raise my feet.

Inside it was dark and cool. It stayed that way if you didn't move anything, even yourself. Once my parents' friend, an old, rich businessman, pulled me into his room, and smoothed his big hands over me. I pushed him hard, as if he was a bureau, and got away. I wasn't supposed to tell. A couple slept in a room off the porch. I came out each day past their rumpled sheets.

When the wash was done and the rooms straight, the youngest daughter, Olympia, carried with her to the beach a portable record player, closed up like a satchel. Sometimes, when she took me with, she made me help set it up on a chair where the sand was damp and the water did its own singing. She wound it and put on her favorites, "Jealousy," "Love Is Where You Find It," "Temptation." She sang a strong contralto and made wide gestures with her arms like the lady who sang on Heinz's pier and gave out pickles. Soon a circle of bored sunbathers pulled up beach towels and chenille bedspreads. Flustered and blushing, I sang too where she asked me to come in. I knew all the words. "Love is where you find it, don't be blinded, it's around you, everywhere."

Frankenstein

EARLY IN THE DAY, A MILLION YEARS LATER AND FROM THE CABIN in the country, I spot that white pyramid, those eggs, each the size of a billiard ball, piled against a pine. Why were they no good to the mother ruffed grouse anymore? Why couldn't she sit them? Had they been corrupted, endangered? She, threatened or called away on urgent business so that it was too late when she returned, they were no longer viable, like children from another marriage?

The fierce grip of a large hand, my fingers are seized so I don't slip away to freedom. My mother and I are walking to the farmer's market. My name is Johnny, I tell the white-bonneted Amish ladies at the produce stands, that's the bellboy who answers the call for Philip Morris cigarettes on the radio, because I wish it was, because I know boys are better. I want the red toque he wears and the outfit of a performing monkey. Maybe my mother is afraid I will wander away to the avenue, but she uses the same firm grip when we go only a couple of doors up from our house to Mrs. Close, her friend who has hung a flag bearing a gold star in the window for a son lost in the War. I am dressed for this visit more formally, in a scratchy brown pinafore, ugliest of all the ugly colors it could be, from the Chubby department of Sears. I go where my mother takes me. I am pulled along like a toy wagon.

I am her creature. I am her Frankenstein monster. She has made me, though she will not make another. I sleep with her in the double bed. She says it's because I'm afraid of the dark but years later, I figure out it's so my father can't sleep here, preventing further slipups. She's too old for a child, she wants to be a lady, and what's more, I have ripped her up inside, which had not been my intention, just to get out.

If I am afraid of the dark, it may be because my parents have taken me to see *Frankenstein*, the movie. Afterwards, they laugh that I hid under the seat the whole time. It is especially dark under there and popcorn and dark blobs of chewing gum are stuck to the floor. But at least I don't have to look at the scary giant who strangles little girls and flees from townspeople who come after him with pitchforks and flaming torches.

Cut-Outs

EARLY ON, BY THE TIME I AM FOUR MAYBE AND ABLE TO LOOK past myself, I know intuitively that each member of my family is living in a trance. My mother is stuck trying to recover from housework and from the ordeal of my birth. Every time she looks at me, she sees something that needs doing, feeding, wiping a nose, smearing icky salve on the red rash where my legs rub each other or on my chubby upper arm that chafes against my body. And so she tries not to look my way. She just sits there on the porch and directs her eyes into the air.

My brother Sidney is in his trance of studying, going over what he is supposed to of what they learn in junior high. He is a very serious student but needs to try to remember what the teacher said and figure out the bad handwriting of the pages of notes he has taken. He tries and tries. And he is in his trance of ignoring me because he doesn't want to be bothered or to have his concentration spoiled, and I am always following after him because he is the only one around the house beside my mother in the daytime.

When the oldest of us, Leo, is home after work and on Saturdays, he is in his trance of listening to Benny Goodman and other big bands or to songs with words on the radio. The words are sometimes funny and hard to understand. He knows that Mairzydoatsanddozydoatsandliddlelamzydivey means, "Mares eat oats and does eat oats and little lambs eat ivy" which he tries to teach me though I usually forget before I get to the end. Mostly Leo is in the trance of wondering what the world holds for him, Leo, out and about with his friends, playing ball or just curious, wandering through the neighborhood. When he goes to the shop to work with my father, cutting diamonds, he's in the trance of learning to be good at it, the trance of wondering if this is what he wants to do, what he will always do, or when my father will fire him.

My father's trance is impenetrable, eternal. I know not to try to get to the bottom of it.

As for me, meanwhile, I am in my trance of wanting. I am so small, what do I yet have, what belongs to me? This particular afternoon, I know what I want without question. I want cut-outs, a cut-out book. On the cover, a lady I see in movies with curls of blond hair swept up on her head. She wears a bathing suit and you push her out of the stiff cover and cut out clothes to fix over her shoulders and around her waist, fastening them with little white tabs. Someone at home will help me cut out the sarongs and evening gowns. How do I know this is what I want? Have I seen this cut-out book in the drugstore when once I went with my mother?

The drugstore is across Franklin Street and around the corner on Lindley Ave.

"Mommy, take me to the drugstore to get cut-outs," I beg and beg.

It's late in the afternoon and everyone will be home for supper soon. Mommy is in her trance of taking a break between the day and the night. She is in her trance of refusal. The more I pull at her skirt, the deeper into it she goes.

"You don't need anything. Go get your crayons Leo bought you, all those colors, go find a coloring book."

But I won't be distracted. Wanting brings tears, folds my hands into grabbing fists. I'm yelling and begging. Mommy, though, will not get up. I know I can cross the street if she watches. She has watched me across before when a ball I throw goes over to the other side or when I want to pick a flower from someone's lawn (and no one is looking). It is like crossing the Atlantic

Ocean, so far and dangerous but it can be done. I can't see the drugstore from here though I can picture the way to it. Down the block past where Bonita with the black sausage curls lives. Her mother has once given me a banana. B is for Bonita and banana. I know the ABC song. It ends with elemenopee and I recognize B when I see it lying down on a page. It looks like a 3 on a stick.

The lawns are high across the street and there are railings that you can use to pull yourself up the stone steps. I never really went that far by myself but I think I can.

At last I can see I am making a dent, wearing Mommy down. Maybe she won't take me but she will give in and give me money to go alone. I see she thinks it's the wrong thing but a little more bawling and chipping away at her could do it. I'm not even sure I feel safe going with no grown-up's hand dangling down to my reach. How far away the drugstore seems and if she said, "No, and that's final!" I'd still snivel but I'd know that was it, that I didn't have to go. But she's worn out. Her nerves are shot, I can see, so press my advantage.

And here it is, the 15¢ she angrily sets into my open palm and closes it over. "Don't lose it."

I look back a couple of times to make sure she is watching, then cross. After Bonita's house, nothing looks familiar. I don't know anyone at this end of the block. I know where the avenue is, though, and keep going. Such a hot day, no one is out on the street. I get to the corner and change direction. I won't have to cross again. The avenue is wide and has fast traffic but I'm safe on the sidewalk.

Because it's late long shadows stripe the street. The grocery store, the alleyway, then there it is, the drugstore with its wide glass windows winking at me. I'm so happy to see it and to know I've come the right way, though I never doubted it, really. I go in. The store is big and the druggist looks surprised to see me there alone. I show him my money and tell him what I want. He's still doubtful but takes me over to the racks of magazines, coloring books, and cut-outs. I pick one up, just what I want. I hand him the money and hold my book tight against me. I go out the door and down the one step to the street.

Triumph! This is how it feels. But I'm scared too. I want to be home with my prize before anything can happen. The sun is still out and the breeze is blowing against my red playsuit. Two children are walking toward me, and I'm glad to see other children out, a little girl my size and a big boy. But I get a little afraid when I see they aren't walking past or around me. They stop right in front of where I am. The boy grabs me. "That's my cut-out book," the girl says. "You stole it from me." And she looks up at her big brother. "That's mine, that's mine!"

I tell them, "No, she's wrong. She's a liar. I just bought this book."

I try to run but there are two of them and one of me. The boy is strong and pins me down. I can't get loose. The girl is scratching at my face with her nails, ripping the book out of my grasp and away from me. No matter how hard I try, I can't hold on to it. I hurt all over where they pull and pummel and scratch. Then my book, bent at the corners and not new anymore, is theirs and they're gone, running around the corner. With dirty hands, I rub the tears out of my eyes and sink to the pavement to catch my breath. I am like a little cat, that close to the ground. All I see is the dark pebbles in the gravel.

It takes a long time before what happened sinks in, before I can stop feeling alternating waves of outrage and pain. Also shame that I can't protect what belongs to me. At last though, I am able to get up. I stand, still wobbly, see where I am and decide the way to go home. I look around to make sure there is nothing worse coming my way. I retrace my steps, all my puffed-up pride drained away. I wail the whole way home. From our porch my mother can hear me down the block. When I get there, will she say it, or will I say it in my mind first? — "See, you were bad. I told you not to go. God punished you!"

Tumblesauce

MY MOTHER STOOD ME UP ON THE DINING ROOM TABLE, THEY
were all big for standing me up on the table, that way they didn't
have to bend to tie my shoe or even put my arms through coat
sleeves, and I stood uplifted, the table becoming my stage, my
pedestal, my shrine and since, long and shiny, it could seat eight,
it was where I learned to roller skate, where I ran and climbed
up when my big brother Sidney was after me for drawing on
the empty flyleaf of his school book, it was paper, wasn't it? it
was blank, oh how they laughed when I entertained them there,
dancing and singing the few songs I knew beginning to end, for
instance: "Pistol-packin' mama, / lay that pistol down, Babe, / lay
that pistol down!" then as a finale, performed the split and the
tumblesauce as Leo had taught me, and once recited a string of
curses I had heard from their own lips and memorized for the
gathered Spartans, Morty, Herb, Stan, Norm, Elliott, his friends
and teammates, "shit, piss, fuck!," while they stood at my feet,
laughing, until Leo shouted, "That's enough!" and smacked me,
and in fact the dining room table was where I was punished for
doing anything bad, like peeling the paint off the kitchen chairs
and eating it or sticking the ruler in the window fan to see if it
was really moving (it didn't seem to be), for there my mother
performed this ritual like an exorcism, or maybe she did it even
preventively, clapping her hands on my shoulders to hold me
still since I'd be slippery, crying and squirming, trying to get out
of her reach, then applying her lips to my forehead like some-
one sucking the venom out of the site of a snakebite to "kiss
the bad away," though sometimes, feeling guilty for something
I had done she didn't yet know about, I climbed up on the ta-

ble myself and begged her, "You have to kiss the bad away," before I could get any peace, anyhow you must understand that the dining room table was not reserved for family dinners, my mother prepared different meals at different times like a restaurant, and we ate separately or just with one other person in the little kitchen the dining room opened onto; for instance, I ate lunch alone at the heel of the kitchen table because everyone was gone in the daytime or sometimes with Eveline who helped my mother clean, Eveline, who I so much loved, the salami or bologna sandwiches meant for her—oh how I longed for her to come each week—I saw her as a kind of reality check, arriving from the world outside looking like ladies in magazines: she wore lipstick, nail polish, and perfume and had on high-heeled shoes and pretty dresses before she changed for flats and work clothes, a housedress like my mother's, and also she told good jokes and said I was "full of soup" even if that wasn't what we were eating, and all day as she dusted or washed the floor, she cracked gum and taught me how, then in the evening if I was lucky enough, I'd sit down to dinner at the same time as Leo who ate steak he had carefully taught my mother to prepare, rib steak, the only kosher kind, best if it squirted blood when stabbed with a fork, or I ate with my father, watching him throw back everything on his plate into his mouth, peas and potatoes and meat on the same forkfuls as fast as he could and chew with his mouth open so both my brothers preferred not to eat with him, yet in all the time I lived at home, I never saw my mother sit down to eat with anyone or alone, though I know she must have eaten because she was fat, and I wondered, could she have made her meals from tasting as she cooked or from leftovers on the plates she gathered to take to the sink as part of clearing the kitchen table and washing up? and I remember Leo asking, "Ginger ale or Black Cherry Wishniak?" when he and I ate together, picking up the right bottle to fill both our glasses though I always answered "Frank's Black Cherry

Wishniak" since I loved that name and could almost taste the sweet, cold bubbles bursting in my throat as I said it, none of us drank water with dinner, just soda as if there was some magic to bubbles, to the gas it pumped up in your belly, after all, gas was freeing, it came back up in a belch like a baby's burp, and the War was over so we could buy soda at the store now and didn't have to rely on what came out of the tap, even if sometimes my parents, like other parents on the street, had deliveries of seltzer in siphon bottles come to our house in a wooden crate, "2 cents plain," they called it, so still a little fancier than water, but old people were the only ones to drink it, and if soda made me belch, that's not the word I'd use, a belch was a "grepsey," what it sounded like to me when I did it, I guess, or else it was Hungarian or a word my mother made up, of course the rest of the family had to learn my baby language so if somersault, as I mentioned, was tumblesauce, everyone I could get to watch me called it that too, and some of them clapped as I looked back between my legs, my lunch churning up inside, and turned my body over my head again and again, the length of the dining room table, into the surprising future.

Everyone Else

STREET PHOTO IN OUR ALBUM: THIS IS THE PERFECT FAMILY I envision, factual, photographed in black and white. They stand in a garden. No, they are arranged before our lawn, dense with grass and dandelions, in the rental house on Franklin Street. My parents are in back, wide and looming. My mother with her high cheekbones, mouth closed on overbite. A smile is inside. She has just taken off the apron she wears in the house. Unexpectedly, there is hair on top of my father's head. How powerful he looks, the center of the group. His hands are down, resting on my two brothers' shoulders. The little one, Sidney, dark and unsure, eyes straining upward, maybe at the unfamiliarity of the touch. As if he has done something wrong and someone has caught him. The unseen photographer? Maybe he is only thinking of doing something wrong. His big brother Leo, beside him, light hair, light eyes, chubby fingers at his sides, smiling, shining, as if nothing he did could ever be wrong.

Never will I see them this way again, this harmonious. I come in so much later it seems an intrusion. No family picture ever includes me. The family is already over.

Where We Are Now

IN THE FIRST, THE RENTED HOUSE IN THE NEW NEIGHBORHOOD, on the new street, we were above a steep lawn and high, stone steps. My mother opens the front door, which is actually situated at the side, facing the door of the adjoining house, and sends me out to play. It is hot summer and I am in white cotton underpants, without a shirt. Only five, I have already grown fat in the shape of breasts. "Shame!" I hear a neighbor call out. I make my way down to the pavement and stand on the street, poking the dirt in the lawn with a stick fallen from a tree. Then I run back up, arms crossed over my chest, feeling other kids, everyone, staring.

Is there another way to act here that we don't yet know? It's like being on the stage. I'd be happy never to make an appearance. I did what I saw my mother do and hoped it was right. She hawked and spit, Ha-tui!, into the gutter and I did too, hearing Kitzie and Mina tittering from their patio, looking down at me over *Photoplay* magazine. I said "comftable" and "beyouteeful," as my mother did before I learned how they were spelled.

Dark House

1946. IT'S TRUE, OPTIMISM IS IN THE AIR. SOLDIERS ARE COMING home from the War and the baby boom is about to start. For the first time since the Depression, my father's business begins to thrive; so many engagements, so many diamond rings. Even at home Daddy is occasionally smiling. As for my mother, she can't take her eyes off a for-sale sign that has sprouted in a lawn across the way. And at last, my parents have their wish, private property, the American dream. At last, they can afford to own.

In the new house I have a room to myself. I could pick out the paper on the walls and I did, pink with a repeating pattern of ladies in long skirts and big hats that I took for princesses. Footmen or messengers presented them with flower bouquets from admirers. There was even my own single maple bed, though everyone's socks and underwear were stored in my bureau drawers.

Like most row houses, the homes on our street rubbed shoulders, so not much light got through, especially on one side. The sun angled in a little but the glassed-in screen porch reflected it back. There are those who believe to this day that ours was the darkest house on the block. Did it seem to someone walking by unoccupied? Would anyone know we were there? Decades later, I meet two boys, now old men, who lived up the block. Neither remembers me, or any of my family. In fact, I begin to doubt us myself. When my old friend, Alvin, and I drive again through the neighborhood after an elementary school reunion and search for it, the house is no longer there. It has burnt down or vanished in some catastrophe, and only a bridge of grass remains between the two neighboring houses.

While we were living in it, ivy hugged the lawn and my mother bought and situated a park bench at the free side, the one closest to the front steps and not connected to the neighbor's lawn. My mother had a fondness for parks, those patches of green in a stone city. She convinced my father to walk miles sometimes, not easy with his limp, so we could all go sit in Burholme Park. It became a Sunday ritual, maybe a reminder of the promenades of gentlefolk she had witnessed in her European childhood.

My mother was nothing if not a lover of fresh air. So I wouldn't be bored, I was encouraged to bring a book, and I took *The Bobbsey Twins* or *The Secret Garden*, also peanuts to feed the squirrels. To my mother, her lawn was an annex of the park. Seated on the bench she felt she was not at home but in a garden, someplace she had purposely come. Many of our neighbors topped off their lawns with stone patios. In the evenings and on weekends, the families sat on matched sets of metal lawn furniture to catch the breeze, but such construction was costly. Also, we wouldn't want to be so much on display. Living in a row house was like riding on a perpetual elevator. You had to nod and say hello when confronted but otherwise tried to keep facing straight ahead so that there'd be a semblance of privacy.

Elementary

OUR MORNING ASSEMBLY THAT WE ENTER MARCHING TO PIANO accompaniment, "The Battle Hymn of the Republic." Our sashes between classrooms opened by strong boys. Our pledge to the flag. Our psalms or Bible passages. Our talents and afflictions: our brilliant one-armed pianist, our wild girl who performs arias in long, yodeling cadences without words. Our disabled principal who leans on a strong boy's shoulder as he addresses us and showers him with spit. Our best student, in short pants so he can strap on his braces. Our President of the whole country who has polio, all our leaders, my father as well, struggling with infirmity. Our single exotic Negro boy, it would be years before there were others, who sits in the last seat of the row next to mine. Our annual Flag Day assembly just after the War when we stand under the hot sun of the schoolyard to sing patriotic songs in loud voices. "From the Halls of Montezuma..." "...when the Caissons go rolling along," and "The Star Spangled Banner," hands over hearts, then end with the elementary school anthem, "Our eyes are on thy waving flag, our hearts in glorious union rise, for Our Dear School," though scarcely anyone knows any more of the words.

Big Streets

"Big Baby! Tell Mama." And Wilma was right, I was a baby. And big. Baby teeth, baby fat. She shoved me into the street between the shoemaker and Harry the tailor. She tricked me with words too. I never thought of what to say back. Empty avenue where Wilma shoved. And maybe a car would come and I'd be dead or at least bounce on the hood as I once saw a little boy do and get up and walk away. The avenues or big streets ran parallel and were bare of trees, whereas on the up-and-down streets of houses, a tree stood in front of each family home, nothing fancy, sycamore, plane (plain?) trees mostly. In between the numbered streets were named ones that carried the city's history, lost to common memory by the time I got to live there. Our street lay between 11th and 12th and Burton or Barton, the vowel changed depending on which corner you were looking at, between 12th and 13th, a little provisional, I thought, the new neighborhood. I walked past rows of houses all the way to and back from school. Everything so even, the lines of streets, the lines of houses, of trees before them, cars in a line parked along the curb.

That was a sunny day when Wilma shoved me, the flat black asphalt stretched endlessly, I might never have gotten across and back home at all if she hadn't pushed.

Yellow Buses

Autumn, I am in grade 1B. All the lower grades are going to a puppet show at Logan Demonstration School. I don't know what a puppet show is or a "demonstration school," for that matter. A puppet, I thought, was Charlie McCarthy and it sat like a wooden baby on someone's lap. And what kind of school? But there has never been a school trip before. I can tell it's important. I can tell it's out of the ordinary, that it signals escape from our places ("Class, get to your places!"). Before I went to school, I imagined pupils were fitted into and chained to the desks. And it is almost true because once installed, we're not allowed to get up.

In the classroom, "the room," Milton Hammer punches my arms black and blue, and I cry in my seat until Mrs. Price grabs him and says, "I will Hammer Milton!" and he stops. I look out through the window and see that big yellow buses have circled up in the schoolyard like a wagon train in a Western. The yard is where we have recess and play games. I am always "it" in Punchinello or dodge ball because I am so big around and so slow. I run out of the ring of children for safety to the row of water fountains situated in a depression in the middle of the yard and stay as long as I can. The water is always on, maybe for ghost children when we are off running and hitting or being hit.

There is universal excitement as I rush out with the others at lunchtime the day of the trip, past the empty buses. All I have to do is go home, eat lunch, then come back to school. And yet something so out of the ordinary seems impossible, beyond my imaginings. My mother doesn't write or read much, but she or someone signed a permission for the trip so it must be going to happen. She will walk me back when it's time, she says.

At the kitchen table, I can scarcely eat my sandwich of lettuce and tomato on white bread, down my glass of milk. Chocolate Tastykake, my favorite, of course, for dessert and I manage to swallow every bite. Then my mother and I listen to her stories on the radio. "Our Gal Sunday," who has a Southern accent, who does everything wrong as "the wife of a wealthy and titled Englishman." It's what can happen even after the happy ending of getting married. I lose myself in the sad episode of Sunday's life though I am listening to time pass too, and all I hear has an echo. Oh, the days that go by in that hour at home. "Hurry, hurry," I tell my mother at 1 p.m. as Sunday makes everything right and we can finally leave. But when we get back to school, though I can't take it in right away, the yellow buses that filled the schoolyard at noon are gone. And I know, I remember, we needed to return 15 minutes early to get on them.

So I never discover what a demonstration school is. I never get to see Punch 'n Judy until I'm 25 years old, and that is in Paris at the Luxembourg Gardens and in another language, under statue-like trees and behind a small circle of little children who are the right age. Maybe I would have cried to watch Punch punch Judy. In my family the father is all bluster, the mother has the ammunition, two solid arms that hit. Maybe I'd have been scared and cried, even, afraid to be on a bus alone. Or bus sick, throwing up, coming and going, I imagine, to make myself feel better. But after, it is always that emptiness of missed buses I feel inside, and in my saddest dreams, the bars of the empty schoolyard I look out through to the rest of my life.

At Night

AFTER WE MOVED THE SECOND TIME, FROM ONE SIDE OF THE
street to the other, I'd sit in the triptych bay window of my par-
ents' room before they came to bed. The tan shades were raised
to half-mast. Street lamps had come on, on the avenue. The
Sinclair and Texaco, one on a corner, were also lit until 11 p.m.
when they closed, so I could see rainbows in the oil-spattered
pavement. Twisting my chair, I watched the trolleys shake and
noisily pass each other, bright inside, people getting on and off
where they stopped at the numbered streets. They didn't stop at
ours. I wondered about the autos and the drivers moving toward
and away from me. Each a secret spirit of the world outside. So
rarely did they turn into our dark street, though I was always
hopeful.

A few neighbors did. For instance, the taxi driver who lived
midway up, he was nice to us children, though his wife scolded
us for all the noise we made. He wore a black jacket and cap
and a black bow tie, his uniform, and parked the cab at the curb
sometimes when his shift was over before driving it back to the
company garage. A dwarf who lived next to him had a car fitted
with special built-up brakes I saw when I looked in once on the
way to school. He didn't have the fairy-tale whimsy of the dwarves
who lived with Snow White; though he too went to work, he nev-
er whistled. But he wasn't mean like Rumpelstiltskin. He was
only a short man who had a little trouble walking, as my father
did, and I felt sad for him.

Watching out the window, what I loved most was the strange-
ness, the purposefulness of the hidden drivers, the ones I couldn't
know. They were going to restaurants or parties in their cars, I

was sure, to New York, maybe even Hollywood. Anyhow, away, away.

My back was to the new maple bedroom suite—twin-bedded, this room, as the motion-picture decency code and my mother demanded. Not the sprawling double bed where the unthinkable once occurred, where I somehow came into being. Alongside, a few feet away, was the battered bureau of a darker finish topped by its lace-edged scarf. A hiccoughing aqua wind-up clock held down one corner. In the center, the cut glass perfume vial and its green-etched stopper. So pretty. The lady next door had given it to me: "I got it when I was a little girl." "Then is it an antique?" I asked. I didn't know that was rude. But she only laughed. My mother, who would have scorned the thing as a *tschochka*, a doodad, decided since it was already here, to make it hers, I would only break it. One other object sat on the bureau scarf, a jar of hand cream, rose-scented, that my mother rubbed into her cracked and housework-red fingers which never healed throughout the winter.

All this is behind me and too real to take into account. I like to pretend nothing exists but unknowable night. I used to be afraid of the dark but now I sit in it gratefully. It's a relief from what the day expects of me, from being watched and tested, feeling I'm doing everything wrong. I keep the lights off, raise the shades that have been lowered at the time the sun sank. The cool glass against my forehead is smooth and comforting. I can see out though no one can see in. Gas stations with their bright signs might intrude on the dark, but the universe presents only at night. There's a moon and what stars come to me, so near the corner. I squint my eyes and the light of the signs and the cars blur, creating a beautiful ribbon of outside, moving and twinkling. The trolleys make a high, chirping noise, the sound I imagine would come from crickets at night in a country field, where I have never been.

Some Things I Know About My Mother

Where she came from was one day's travel from Vienna
as she hid in the hay of her father's wagon,   staring out
at rich people and soldiers   when he found her he let her
sit up front and boss the donkey   they stopped to warm
themselves at the fires of gypsies   at eleven she made a
long journey alone   she was pulled along on the strength
of promises   and found herself without a voice yet on new
ground   in a boarding house on Hester Street   she lit the
stove and emptied slops   she was always cold   she married
a loud voice, a strong smell, a pipe   a man with children
older than herself   she ran away   in a factory she sewed the
hems of handkerchiefs   cousins took her in   imagine their
evenings filled with long Yiddish vowels   Nany, the mother,
hung little crocheted baskets in her room   she cooked for them
and sewed herself a dancing dress   what she loved more than
anything was to dance   the Charleston, the two-step, bound to
a partner or spinning free   small feet across the smooth floor,
no accent stumbling after her   at sixteen, a photograph: she
and her sister in sailor dresses tinted blue   her cheeks are red,
her hair, white blond   there is the lifelong space between her
teeth   later, her sister will marry a farmer, her brother become a
grocer so his family can eat   while she dances at Roseland every
night   a man she likes will never dance with her   at nine he
fell, becoming lame   a diamond cutter   he learned his trade
in an orphanage   for hours he sits, examining the brilliant
facets for a flaw,   the way he looks at everything   they met
at Coney Island   in two weeks they were married   the next

time she danced was with her grown son at his wedding   her
feet were still sure   as they waltzed, she waved a hand in the
air   describing the same graceful triangle again and again

Cousin Jo

HOW MANY TIMES GROWING UP DID I ACTUALLY SEE HER? HALF A
dozen? But how important she was in my life, my New England
cousin, Jo. And those early meetings lasted for days while she
visited my family on her summer vacation. She was a school
teacher, first in an immigrant family to go to college, and during
the Depression, against all odds. An American story; it could
have been a movie: collapsing farmhouse, miles to the one-room
school, shoes with holes and newspaper linings, the one dress
washed and ironed every couple of days, the father who wants to
keep her home to help in the kitchen.

I tagged after her on her visits, affection-starved, hero-wor-
shipping. I loved the soap that smelled like her skin, that flawless,
beautiful complexion she had till she was nearly 100. Avaderma,
not perfumed but clean-smelling, moistened with olive oil, pure.
She gave me a bar.

Jo, who knew children and liked them, so whole a person
in herself that she had something left over to give, kindness,
warmth. I was used to my mother's weary inattention, too many
years of children, her free-floating anxiety, one corner of a thing
on her mind masked down while another loosened and came up:
crumbs, *schmutz*, danger. The worn table top, the sink with juice
stains. The wind outside that some days took her breath away.
Escalators. She'd admire Jo, wish to be like her again, young
and brave.

For Jo was a traveler, as I hoped to be as soon as I was allowed.
Miami or the Caribbean if she could afford it, Philadelphia, with
us, if not. Philadelphia anyway, alighting here going south, like
a butterfly migrating. There was the War and no one went to

Europe except soldiers, and now after, the place was a shambles not a tourist destination. What was left but battlefields and mortar-scarred house fronts, my parents said, and who would want to go back anyway? It had been hard enough to get out of there.

Jo's hair was thick and brown, as was mine then. She wore it shoulder-length, with a side pompadour secured by a hairpin or barrette. Everything about her a little asymmetrical, the peplum on a dress or blouse that pulled a little crimped pouch of the material off to the side. The cast in one of her dark, almond eyes, not so much a distraction as a point of interest. Her disarming remarks. Just after my first period, for instance, she took me aside. "Now you must never let a boy pull your pants down." As if I had been in the habit of doing that before.

Two girl cousins, we were, from households of boys; she had three brothers and I, two. Just another girl though the age difference could have made her my mother. Wouldn't that have been grand? In a photo taken when I am seven, we are seated on the wooden kitchen steps going down to the alley. I am stretching my legs out with scabbed knees to reach the same step she did in her pretty open-toed high-heels. We are both in best dresses, hers, dark and formal, mine white satin that I wore for dress up, a print of flower bouquets.

Jessie is coming! my mother would croon excitedly in the hours before my cousin's arrival, scurrying around the house to pick up and regroup displaced objects. I knew she preferred to be called Jo, though, short form of Josephine, her given name, but also I thought for the heroine of the very American *Little Women*. If she was known in the family as Jessie, it would have been how her mother, Aunt Hannah, in her Hungarian accent, pronounced Josie. Jo's visits always came with presents, the family gift, chocolates or glazed dried fruit, which, little glutton that I was, I couldn't keep my hands off. And for me alone, she brought jewelry, bubble bath and powder, treasured if sometimes unread books, *Alice in Wonderland, Huckleberry Finn,* in beautiful, illustrated editions. Once, a collection of Bible stories. Then one gift so mysterious and beautiful it was new to me each time I looked. It was a pendant set in mother of pearl, the scene, a desert island anchored by a palm tree swaying under a dark turquoise sky, the smile of a moon. A convex glass cap magnified and added a dimension. I dreamed of the place, it had to exist somewhere where Jo had bought it, and the mustached men she might have danced with there.

The pendant dangled from a delicate chain and could also be worn as a pin. Was I so careless a child? Maybe it was inevitable, but the chain soon broke. I pinned it then to a yellow blouse, just at the side of the Peter-Pan collar. When the pin mechanism itself snapped off in my clumsy haste to put the thing on, I saved the little scene just to hold in my hand and look at. Then my brother Sidney, who was known to be "handy," offered to fix it for me. "I'll solder it together," he told me. I gave it over gratefully. Half an hour later, he came up from the basement with a lead slug in his hand, that nervous laugh of his telling me before I saw, that something had gone horribly wrong. "It melted," he said. Although I knew he had only been trying to help, not to have the pretty pendant, even to hold and look at was like losing a real place I could never go to again.

Immigrant Aid

NOT LONG AGO, I'M PRESENTED WITH A DOCUMENT, MY MOTHER'S naturalization papers, dated 1943, salvaged from my brother Sidney's belongings after he too is gone.

Here is my mother, as young as I ever remember. Four feet eleven inches tall. Was she really so small and yet so formidable? Hair: brown, streaked with gray, Eyes: hazel. Of course, they weren't. But the kind of piercing green that guesses everything, that make you eager to look away. And 1943, when she'd already been in the country 32 years. What of the citizenship classes I have been told she attended as a young girl where she learned to speak with no accent and acquired a rudimentary ability to read and write English? Likely, her only schooling. By 1943, though, the world knows that the Nazis are set on exterminating all the Jews of Europe. Is she afraid she could still be deported? She would want to make sure, to prove that it's official, that she is a documented citizen and can't be sent back.

Then too, something comes to me, something I remember from childhood. A trip to New York when we weren't visiting relatives. I was very little, not a toddler but old enough to take along because there is no one to leave me with. Or because she wants to show she has an American child. I'd be six at least, so a few years after the certificate of naturalization. The name of the agency comes back, not a name at all but letters, an acronym. We are going to HIAS, the Hebrew Immigrant Aid Society. The big war is over.

My mother's family in Hungary is mostly dead, certainly the few left, dispersed; D.P.'s, displaced persons, they are called. Whoever remains, she is trying to find, maybe has started to search for even during the war. She wants to get them out, any younger brothers and sisters left, to have them here, safe. Not the children of her mother, Esther, they are here—herself, and Aunt Hannah, and Uncle Sam, head of the little family, who preceded his sisters and advanced the money for their passage. But the stepmother's children, the evil stepmother who starved and beat her. "She was too young. She didn't know what she was doing."

We are climbing up, up, in an elevator, a fast one. My pigtails are pulled tight enough to make me cry and secured with red ribbons. The little moving room is pulling me apart, up out of myself. My ears hurt. My stomach lurches. Shouldn't my mother be concerned? I yank at her dress but she doesn't pay attention. Who will save me? Her mind is on them, the lost ones. Her eyes are moist. I don't think it's the wind outside. She never likes the wind, she's afraid of it, she can't catch her breath. And it's winter. New York is colder by a few degrees than Philadelphia, where we live. If I thought to look more closely, though, I'd see she is crying.

We are here to beg for her relatives. Aunt Helena with dark hair but the same space my mother and I both have between our front teeth, Uncle Joseph, who may be in Palestine, anyone else alive after the Nazi death camps, and she doesn't have faith it will work. My father, that nervous, hurried man, who hardly ever talks but who is kind to me, who I tell when my mother hits me and who yells at her, won't pay the $500 bond that must be put up by a U.S. citizen to guarantee visas for immigrants. For him, every day is a war, going out and making a living, fighting business rivals, fighting for business. De-mobbed servicemen are coming back to sweethearts, buying diamonds he cuts for engagement rings. My mother saved us when he could find no work after the Depression, and the family lived in a slum apartment house where she was janitor. One day I will realize that both my parents are afraid of losing everything. That what they are doing, living their lives, raising a family, might somehow be illegal or become so, and all they have taken away.

My father won't pay for the visas, won't even show his financial records. No one can see how much he makes. It will be the same years from now when the Merit scholarship committee my last semester of high school also wants to know his income and he refuses to tell. But now it's because his wife's relations, "Greenhorns," will "expect a handout," and he has worked too hard for what he has to part with any of it.

How can I make my mother believe in the pain in my ears? Maybe it will never go away. But the elevator is opening. We have arrived on a high floor in this tall building. I'm sick to my stomach when I remember how big it looked from outside. Maybe we are at the very top. I stumble, not quite able to feel the still ground suddenly underfoot. Then she is pulling me by my hand down a long corridor with marble walls, opening a door of wood and pebbled glass, and sitting me down on a hard wooden chair.

A sign is stenciled on the door: HIAS. "Is this right?" I ask her. "It's just letters."

"It's right. It's where they help people come over from the other side," she tells me.

She unbuttons first my red winter coat then her heavy black one with the tacked on Persian lamb collar, her good one, hardly ever worn. The receptionist at last takes note of us. We are motioned forward and push through the swinging half-door to her. My mother says why we are here, and we are allowed to go on into the inner sanctum. The man we have come to see is here and he has us sit before his desk. My mother takes out her papers (maybe the naturalization certificate is one). He is not impatient. He looks at them and doesn't holler at us if this is what my mother expects. He is, in fact, nice. He looks at everything. He asks questions, then he talks. "I can help you. I want to help you. It's my job to help you. But your husband has got to sign the bond. It's the only way we can go forward."

Leaving, we are both sad. I feel bad because my mother feels bad. And something else too, shame or guilt. Not because I have or could have done anything, I know that, but because I am my father's daughter. He is wrong yet I forgive him. I love him. For my own survival, he will remain dear to me, dearer than these unknown relatives I pity whose blood I also share.

Chicken

KITCHEN. CHICKEN. HOW ALIKE THEY SOUND. THE BABY CAN'T imagine one without the other. The kitchen is where Mommy lives and the Baby knows to look for her there. "Mommy! Mommy!" she cries as she runs in from the dark, empty rest of the house. And there she finds her and also the horror of the dead chicken left koshering on the drain board of the sink. It's Friday and all its blood has to run out so it can be cooked for Shabbos dinner.

Linoleum patterns the kitchen floor with big squares that improbable pink flowers are floating in, though black patches have been scrubbed out of it over the years. Once the Baby thought you could pick pieces of sunlight up off the floor, though she was never quick enough. The kitchen is her playpen. Mommy continues to cook or iron as she sits the Baby down on the floor before the sink and takes out the big pot and the little pot and some wooden spoons for her to play with. With a hollow, dull thud, the Baby hits the outsides and hisses circles around the insides of the pans, as if she too were cooking. When she is tall enough, the Baby can pull herself up to standing by holding onto the edge of the sink. When she eats standing up like that, Mommy will say, "You dasn't get crumbs!" and make her finish her bread and butter leaning over the sink.

Farther into the room is the kitchen table, a slick red and white-checkered oilcloth spread over it. The table has its head against the wall. Boxes of cereal, salt, and sugar in a glass bowl are set here, whatever doesn't fit in the cabinets above. Only the bottom is available and that belongs to whoever is eating at the time. The family comes and goes when they're home, Mommy making different food for them all the time. The bottom of the table is where she, the Baby, sits down now with a white-bread sandwich on her plate. "Do you want an eggie?" Mommy asks, but the Baby doesn't.

A little white enamel table, worn because it has been everywhere the family ever lived, is by the sink. Mommy cuts vegetables here and makes crusts for pies. She takes up a big rolling pin and rolls and rolls. The silky dough flattens as wide as a pillowcase, so elastic it folds over the wooden pin without sticking. The Baby likes to stay nearby. Delicious leftover dough sprinkled with sugar and cinnamon goes into the oven after, specially for the Baby. In the table's single drawer is the silver they give out at the movies, a whole set though they don't really match. On Tuesday, ironing day, because Monday is washday, blankets and sheets are wadded up and spread over the enamel table for the hot, heavy iron to go over, smoothing wrinkles out of hankies and shirts and pinafores. The Baby knows how hot the iron can get because it made her cry out when she once touched it. The dark shape of a triangle marks the top sheet because Mommy stopped and set the iron down once in a hurry when something was boiling over on the stove.

At the right side of the room is an open door and the curved stairway to the cellar where the icebox is kept, stairs the Baby fell down rocking the little wooden chair Daddy bought her. Later, a refrigerator with a pebbled surface will be wedged between cellar and pantry doors and, in their old age, Mommy will store in it the lamb stew or chicken soup meant for half a week's dinners, fat congealing on the surface and oiling her and Daddy's lips after it's heated, and the strong iceman will no longer be needed to heft a block of ice downstairs on his shoulders.

This afternoon as she runs in, the Baby tries to ignore the salted chicken on the drain board in its pimpled skin, blood running down the drain. When Mommy first takes apart the brown butcher paper, golden eggs are exposed, like glazed-over eyes that stare up at her, and giblets in their shiny tubes of guts. It has been explained that the eggs could have been born as chicks if the mother hen was not killed to make supper.

Before the horror of the Shriners parade the Baby never knew where supper came from. That day, and Mommy took her, a giant chicken with yellow and red feathers pranced down the street. But something was wrong. Something was missing. No eyes or beak, just flapping wings and feet going in two directions and a fat body in between. "Where is its head?" Gone, she suddenly realized, and felt for her own head as if it too might detach. She began to cry. "Stop it. You're a big girl now," Mommy said. "It's only a man in a chicken suit." And the Baby knew she had been tricked about where supper came from all of her life so far.

Mommy had a lot to do with chickens. Once she twirled one around her head three times. It was supposed to be alive to take on all the sins of the year at Yom Kippur, but she bought a dead one from the butcher and used that instead. In their old house, Mommy had a live chicken as a pet, but that was before the Baby was born, and she was sorry she never got to see it. She was told it laid dainty brown eggs and lived in the backyard. A little red Bantam hen, and friendly, and its name was Banty. It ate corn from Mommy's hand. But it used to get out and scratch in the neighbors' lawns. They complained, this was the city, she didn't live in a *shtetl* anymore, and Mommy had to send it away.

An odor of percolated coffee, raw fowl, even linoleum polish is thick in the air of the kitchen. And in the rain, the smell of softened paint on the white wooden chairs that you can scrape and pill with your fingertips. A slop bucket is under the sink where juiced orange halves are thrown after breakfast and later, the parts of the chicken they don't eat, bills, feet, feathers. The Baby doesn't like the odors from this bin and tries never to be around when it is opened.

The dregs of coffee are part of the bad smell in the bin. But early in the day the coffee has a delicious aroma. It's what the Baby rises to. A coffee grinder is mounted on the wall of the attached, unheated pantry. Mommy wears Leo's red Spartans baseball jacket to go in there to grind the beans. The sound as she turns the handle of the grinder is often enough to wake the Baby from her second-floor bedroom, without Mommy needing to come and shake her out of sleep. The pantry, sometimes called the shed, is an overhang with gray-green shingles, and the door has to be locked because from it wooden steps lead down to the alleyway shared with the back of 11th Street.

The Baby can stand on a stool, look out the narrow window, and see into other people's pantries. At night when only dark is out there she is afraid of robbers entering secretly while the house is asleep, also ghosts or monsters. Even in the day, just a knock will scare her, but it's only ever the neighbor next door needing something, or a peddler. For horse-drawn carts pass through the alley, and the loud cheerful voices of produce sellers hawking their wares, "Hey, I got fresh spinach, fresh tomato!" Or umbrella fixers who also sharpen kitchen knives on a big sparking wheel the Baby mustn't get close to. One of the family's two milkmen, Abbott, also comes down the back alley with his wagon and clomping white horse.

But there is another milkman who comes on other days to the street in front in the blue, early light. He drives a truck and parks it at the corner. Then he walks up the block, swinging the metal cage of glass milk bottles, and whistling so no one thinks he is a robber. "Yo, Martin!" Mommy calls in her loudest voice to get his attention and make him stop and bring us ours, topped with its plug of yellow cream, or to take away the rinsed empty bottles from earlier in the week. Otherwise, if she doesn't see him, she will leave empties on the top step, and he will make a trade.

For a long time, the Baby thinks the name of the milkman is Martin. But one day he pulls up before their house in his clean white truck. By then she can read a little and sees that Martin is the name on the side of the truck, and that it stands for the company that makes the milk. Anyhow, this milkman has brown eyes and crew-cut brown hair. He wears a jacket and pants the white color of milk, and looks just like the chiseled wooden peg of a milkman who fits in the milk truck passed on to her from a neighbor boy. He is a neat, pleasant, perfectly shaped man like the toy figure. He is what Mommy calls "fine," meaning very American-looking.

Because she trusted him, it was Martin Mommy asked to take her pet hen back to the farm where the milk cows are kept. Anyhow, Banty would have been too small to make much of a meal, so maybe she did get to the country and they allowed her to scratch and run around a big field in exchange for her little brown eggs. The Baby likes to think of her there still, living out her life.

The stove beside the enamel table, the one tonight's chicken will cook in, is also white enamel. It is old-fashioned, potbellied like a fat person, with black burners, and it burps and the gas hisses when Mommy turns it on. A few times, the Baby remembers, when Daddy has been gone for a long time and Mommy doesn't know if he's ever coming back, or if the Baby has been very bad, Mommy runs to the stove with tears in her eyes. She says she will stick her head in the oven, "take the pipe," as she puts it, and opens the door wide and does. The Baby doesn't know what to do.

But then Mommy calms and pulls herself out of the oven without turning the dial.

Family Business

A DIAMOND. HARDEST KNOWN SUBSTANCE. USED AS AN ABRASIVE or a cutting tool in industry, even to play phonograph records.

The trade of the diamond cutter is passed down through generations. It has a medieval aura; one thinks of Dutch gem cutters of the 17th century, rows of houses fronting canals, glinting windows you can't see past. It's a secretive business, best kept within the family. It has risks. The product, even in the beginning stages, found like gravel in a mine or a stream by wretchedly treated African miners, is a rough stone that looks most like a lump of crystallized sugar yet can be worth thousands of dollars. Despite this, my family will never be rich. A diamond doesn't belong to the cutter. He, like the miner, is only an intermediary. The stone passes through his hands; it's his labor that determines his living. The finished product accrues value as the result of his work and the risks he takes, and is sold to a dealer or the rare private party as soon as possible. Wrapped in shiny paper folded to two-inch squares, the parcel of stones can be slipped into a breast or pants pocket and carried on his person along busy streets, on a subway or any kind of public transportation. On the street, he'd be circumspect, wary, eyes straight ahead, taking note of everyone passing yet trying to escape their notice.

I say "he" because cutting is traditionally a man's profession. I was the only one of my father's children never employed in his business, not even part-time after school as both my brothers were. It was a dirty trade, my father said, not "fine" enough for a girl. I couldn't even keep the books, which Leo, in his precise and beautiful hand, did so painstakingly well. There was another reason I may not have been taken into the business. My father wouldn't want me to know the sums involved since I was so young, and a girl, and might be indiscreet.

And if I write, if I cut and slash, disinter flaws in my life and my family in a thousand poems, in the words I set down here, am I not being indiscreet? Yet I use the model of my father. I follow his procedure, share his concerns. A diamond is carbon, as a pencil is. Graphite too, compressed in the earth, the product of pressure and heat. The girdle, the culet, the multiple sides, a diamond itself is a revelation. It is a hall of mirrors, each facet shining into another to reflect back the light that's trapped inside, light that breaks up like a prism into all the colors there are. Diamond. To start, it must be struck at an angle, the cleavage grain. I can imagine the terror of beginning.

All together, diamonds were my father's fortune and misfortune. Chips flying off the wheel in the process of being cut, the rare stone the size of the nail on someone's pinky dropped and lost between floor tiles. Not to mention fear of being followed from his place of business and ambushed. My father worried about robbery, about the "Syndicate," even about covetous neighbors. At home one night I answered a phone call from a man who identified himself as an FBI agent, perhaps my father's very own designated FBI agent.

Once Daddy disappeared for days. His gut maybe told him he wasn't safe. People were after him, could be the mob. This is how I imagined it. He'd hurried to the subway, turning his head over his shoulder at every footstep behind him, sure he was being followed. He got to Market Street and thought it better to grab a cab to the train station. The Silver Meteor was the first train out and was going sufficiently far away, to Florida, so he booked on it. Twelve hours later he was in Jacksonville and again the extravagance of a taxi because he couldn't afford to waste time.

Sweating in his winter-weight suit, he'd stop at the first decent-looking hotel, not glancing right or left as he finished signing in at the desk—did he give his real name?—and went through the lobby, trying not to attract attention. In the small, plain room, he unpacked quickly and settled in. Later, much later, calm and feeling the need to eat something, he pulled aside the flimsy lace curtain at the window, sure he had seen before a sailor who stood across the street, that the fellow had been tailing him and was waiting. He wouldn't go out before dark and wouldn't come home to us for days until things seemed quiet and the street below was clear.

A diamond. Every day my father, and later my brother Leo beside him, batters against the obdurate surface. With each raw stone, he invents a strategy, an incision that goes straight to the brilliant heart and does not shatter it. Acid too is used.

Held to the window, the fire of the gem catches the natural light and comes to life. "A perfect stone. Ain't it a beauty?" my father says to us with pride, a rare grin. "It could knock your eye out." He's making a square-cut engagement ring for Cousin Jo who has come all the way from New England to pick out a stone. Daddy wants her to be happy with it and is even more exacting than usual. I have come down to the shop with her, one of my rare visits here. I remember how strong my father seems, sleeves rolled up, his muscular forearms with black hair standing up like wire.

On rainy or cloudy days, he and my brother are trapped in the stuffy, small room. At 12:30 Leo at least goes out. He's free for half an hour to get a sandwich, a malt, shoot the breeze at one of the narrow lunch places, everything small, claustrophobic, on the gray, one-block street, allowing only so much sky. Seventh to Eighth, Sansom runs, the numbered streets dead-ending it on either side, making a little pocket of it. The buildings that started out as a row, by this time are marked by individual touches, different heights and colors, some fused to make a larger down-stairs business. Leo joins the knots of other young men loitering in dark doorways like miners let up at last from the shaft, eyes to the passing scene, dazzled by sunlight.

Flaws, Faults

As a cutter, my father used acid to get rid of a flaw. The stone sometimes grew around one. That was the danger, though he hoped he could guess right, using instinct and his jeweler's loupe. If it was just a corner, a speck, acid did the trick.

He was alert to the flaws in us too. Maybe we were good at heart. We were his so must be. As a kid Leo though disappointed him. He was a bum. He played ball after school when he should have been studying, like Sidney. He laughed too much with his friends. Went out, God knew where, at night. And I, I believed people. If someone said they would come over to play and didn't show, I cried to spend the afternoon alone. I expected other kids to like me and was hurt most when they made fun of me for being fat or punched me on the way home from school. The crying couch, I thought of it, where I lay alone in the living room. Red mohair, soft, a comfort, but also a prickly reminder.

"Only your mother and your father love you. No one else gives a damn." That had been his experience. My mother was sociable, she liked company. She went to Mrs. Holzer's two doors down or asked in the Old Lady from the next block for tea. Daddy thought she talked too much, confided too much to the neighbors. "What is it their business?" The whole bunch of us, he said, were too trusting.

Daddy also told me I had no right to complain. Then the tenement and the rats came into it and I'd feel even worse. I thought of his limp and how hard he worked and his wretched childhood, all of them huddled together with little heat and sometimes no food. So did I have any reason to be unhappy?

There'd be the acid sting too, when in eighth grade I showed him our elementary school graduation picture, with me centered in the first row. I had been elected vice president. "Look at that pretty kid," my father said and as I started to smile, I saw he was pointing not to me but at another girl three rows behind.

Later, as a teenager, I'll tell him my ambition: to be a writer. "Only one in a million makes it," he says. But he surprises me a few years later when he agrees to take me to a notary to prove my age so I can enter poems in a *Seventeen* magazine contest.

So if a diamond is the hardest natural substance while graphite is among the most malleable, it was a little like my father and me. Both are forms of the carbon atom, in the same family, so to speak. A diamond is transparent, a pencil mark, opaque. I think how a pencil is my writing instrument of choice though because it can be erased. You can change your mind. It streaks along paper, plant on plant. A diamond, they say, lasts forever, but so too, I'd wanted to tell him, does some writing.

MY PARENTS NEVER GO OUT
WITHOUT ME

Previous page: Mom and friend dressed up, circa 1920.

Left Behind

MY PARENTS NEVER GO OUT WITHOUT ME. ONE NIGHT THEY SAY that is just what they are doing, going out. They have joined a lodge that celebrates festive occasions throughout the year. They pay dues and this entitles them to burial plots and various dinners while they are alive which they must pay for additionally. My mother is in a black dress, my father wears his one blue suit and a tie. She has placed a dab of lipstick on her mouth and used her little finger to spread it around. It's still kind of spotty. He carries his gray fedora before him. They look dressed up, the way they do when we are all going to a wedding.

They are square and stolid, leaning to one side as they stand there in the living room, close to the door, like the people in the *New Yorker* cartoons that now remind me of them. I am lying on the red mohair couch, feeling betrayed, crying my heart out. "You're leaving? I can't believe it! Who will take care of me?" I don't know how long they will be gone. I don't know what a lodge is or who else belongs, except that there will be food and that it is for grownups. Whatever it is, I am meant to be left behind, like the furniture. And what's more, they don't really know how to do this "going out." There is no baby-sitter, no phone number for emergencies. "Sidney will be home soon. He'll stay with you." My God, left alone and all I can look forward to is torments devised by my big brother, who is not even home? It is insupportable! I am beside myself.

The tears continue. My parents stand where they are, unsure. My father is first to turn around. Then they both go upstairs, a little shamefacedly, to put on the old clothes they wear around the house. Of course I feel guilty, a spoiler, though no one says that, but also justified, also relieved. They never try to do this again, to see if after the first shock, I might become resigned. The only thing they get out of the lodge, after all, is the burial plots.

Jealousy

1.

I was born to it although I didn't know. It was the title of a popular song I heard on the radio when I was little that the big girls, the jump-rope girls sang, seated on the stoop awaiting their turns, "Jealousy." Only, "Leprosy" is what they sang. Sandy, with the blue plastic glasses and frizz of blond hair, was on the top step, and there was Tillie and Kitzie, below. "Leprosy, it's crawling all over me. There goes my left foot, there goes my right foot. I sometimes wonder, the spell I am under..."

In my family, my mother was jealous of all that my father coveted apart from her, boxing matches and ball games. Chocolate ice cream. The schnapps downed in a gulp at a wedding before she could prevent it. Even the plump blond across the way he doffed his hat to. Most of all it seemed, of me, her daughter too. "He wanted you. I was all finished. The boys were already grown." How embarrassing to find herself pregnant again at 40. What could she say to people? So I could see, right from the beginning, I was *de trop*. I thought if he wanted me, she maybe didn't. She was jealous of the way he might look at me and laugh with pleasure, that odd, sideways laugh he didn't do often. Of how much, he said, I looked like his dead mother.

My father was jealous of the milkmen, there were two, that my mother waited for in the morning, each requiring separate delivery instructions on alternate days: whole milk, homogenized, and cream from Abbott's. Buttermilk, eggs, too, brought by Martin, not the milkman's name but the name of the company, who

87

delivered from a farm, not a bottling plant. There were also the iceman, the coal man, peddlers, the Fuller Brush man, most of whom my father never saw, for he went to work early. But he conjured them in his imaginings. Once, this was when the family was still in the Bronx before the Depression, before they came to Philadelphia, before me, Aunt Eva told me, he tried to enlist his brothers in a plan to waylay and beat up the plumber my mother spoke to on long afternoons, out of necessity, out of isolation, and the wish to have the drain repaired.

Sidney, the second son, squeezed in the middle between our big brother, Leo, almost a grown-up, and me, the new baby, sandwiched between envies. At ten, another child appears. My mother nurses, nurses, until I am nearly three so she won't get pregnant again. She and I sleep in a big bed with a flowered metal headboard, maybe for the same reason. Sidney makes fun of me for being such a baby. Well, it's not my idea. Water must be boiled so I don't get sick. When I am sick, my mother is on 24-hour watch. Oh, the shame of having a baby die on you! It doesn't get better for him. Sidney will never have access to the pudding spoon to lick anymore. And he is too big for anyone to take on their lap.

Did it go the other way too, was Sidney jealous of Leo? They shared a room, a room though not much else. I wondered what they said to one another, from the twin beds that matched our parents', in those moments before sleep. Afternoons, Leo rushed off to meet the Spartans, his friends from childhood, in the schoolyard to play whatever game of ball was in season. I believe Sidney loved Leo more than anyone; when we're all old, and Leo is in a dementia beyond recall, Sidney says Leo is, has always been, an angel. As a teenager, he'd have wished for his brother's ease and nonchalance, the way girls smiled to get Leo's attention. For Leo's elegant handwriting or his natural athletic ability, his skill at cutting diamonds when they both went down to the shop after school to work for my father. Mostly, how Leo seemed to get what he wanted without half trying. Maybe I saw before Sidney did that Leo wisely never wanted what he couldn't get.

The schoolyard surrounded Birney school, where the Spartans had met in second grade and Leo found the name for them, a kind of sports franchise. Afterwards, my mother wore the red team jacket to hang wash outside and to shovel coal in. Sidney trailed after the Spartans on their after-school excursions, with me in tow because he was the designated baby-sitter. He wanted to please my mother, to be the good boy, not the crybaby that I was. The schoolyard had a basketball court and white circles painted on cement for games I couldn't even fathom. It seemed its own world, at least a mile across. Iron bars surrounded it.

The swings hung on chains and were off to the side like small gallows. I'd be deposited forlornly in the box of a baby swing, strapped in. I had to stay where I was put and hope someone passing would feel moved to push me while Sidney drifted over to the basketball court in case Leo and the other boys invited him to sink a basket. Was Leo jealous of Sidney? I didn't think so. He knew who had the upper hand. He could afford to be magnanimous.

2.

I am jealous of the big girls. They don't let me jump Double Dutch with them, not that I'd dare. I know I'm not fast enough, the long rope will cut into my thighs or I'll trip. I pass by and look and smile, stand for a bit and watch. They don't invite me to join them on the steps, either. They are so pretty. They whisper among themselves and say things out loud I don't understand. I am jealous too of Rebecca up the street. She is my age, but her mother fusses over her to make her pretty and oils her hair so it will shine.

I am jealous of other children's mothers who wear perfume and have wardrobes for work and don't come in housedresses to pick up their children from school. Once a classmate says, "Your grandmother is waiting for you over there," pointing to the schoolyard fence, and I don't bother telling him, "No, it's my mother, she's just old, she doesn't dye her hair." I am jealous most, of course, of my mother. She is co-equal with my father in power, more powerful actually for she controls the house, where I spend most of my time. She makes the rules my father can't be bothered with. And sometimes, even when I report to him her injustices, the fights we have, the slaps, he takes her side. Later, when I'm allowed out by myself, I go with trepidation, a vague sense I may have misplaced something. Would I find again where I lived, treading among the identical houses?

All this time, I am jealous that my brothers, "the Boys," can go off on their own, without anyone to mind them, that they can leave the house and my mother's sharp eyes, whereas my hand has to be in the prison of her hand whenever I go out. Many, many things to be jealous of. I let the bitterness out in increments. That way it poisons nobody, no one notices or maybe even cares. A sudden quietness. A stomp upstairs. The object in my hand slammed down. An audible, indrawn breath.

I am jealous of the mysterious back room where each of my brothers has his own bed. I'm jealous of their time together. I am jealous of the long table set aside for Sidney where he studies in my parents' bedroom. He shuts himself away there every afternoon after school under three wide windows, for the natural light and the privacy. I can imagine my parents bargaining for that table, extracting it from the jumble of old junk at one of the used furniture stores on Girard Avenue. They'd see it as an investment on his path to college and their dream for him of medical school. I'm not allowed to make a sound while he studies. "Are we fighting again, girls?" he yells down when my mother and I spoil his concentration, one of many unspecified protocols like life at court.

Any flat surface is a good enough desk for me, my homework mostly done on oilcloth laid over the kitchen table beside cereal boxes and condiments. I am jealous of how my mother looks at Sidney, with something I guess is pride. Of how both my brothers sit with the men at synagogue on holidays, in the place of importance near the Ark, not hidden away on a balcony with the women. I hate who I am as well as how I am treated. How many things can be outright spoiled for me because they aren't perfect, like the smudged page of homework I have to turn in, result of a leaky pen? Sometimes I think of the time before me, before I intruded on what I believe to be an ideal family.

My life at this stage, even at home, is made up of lessons. School might be 24 hours a day. Sometimes I fail and don't know what I've done wrong. In fact, I seem not to have done anything, only be myself. At seven, I like to draw and sometimes I'm someplace with no crayons when the urge comes on, so I have to use pencil and pretend the world is black and white like the movies. Pencil is more exact but I miss the particularity of color, so like the real world, and the fifty-crayon Crayola box Leo bought for me, with flesh color, salmon, yellow-green, lavender—although I have trouble telling this from gray, a problem I still have in certain light as an adult. What I draw on depends on what's at hand. I've been severely discouraged from using the wall even though walls seem always to surround me. I like the backs of photos, like my second-grade Halloween picture, but they are few. Or the flyleaves of books. These don't have any other use that I can see. Nothing printed on them to read.

Any books in the house though are likely to be Sidney's, for school or reading. Usually, I pull the blank pages out because

I can understand he might not like the pictures I make. Sometimes, though, the impulse is too strong and I don't want to take the time, so I draw right in the book. What you'd call pastorals, usually. Flowers in fields, not that I have ever been in a field, and a little girl, probably myself, who smiles and dances under the perfect, round circle of the sun. Wherever the pictures turn up, and Sidney finds them, he is not pleased. Anger is his response, and revenge. But revenge is never equal. It's meant to teach a lesson and needs to be notched up. So I'll find a favorite book, of the three I own, torn and inked over, worst, the book about the princess's five beautiful gowns shown in color illustrations. Then there'll be shouting and crying and escalating violence and bad feeling. The final insult, ink he's splashed on my white, satin party dress.

3.

Once, years later, Leo and I are walking side by side. By then I am a teenager. We have left the house in one another's company. Probably it is just chance that has taken us in the same direction, toward Broad and Olney, B & O, as it has since come to be known, the way Kensington and Allegheny were paired while I was growing up—an intersection, a transportation hub—and finally reduced to K & A. (Leo's friend Donald opened a diner there in the '70s. I remember delicious greasy donuts, a quick breakfast I shared with Leo at the El when I had spent the night at his house with his new family. But the time I'm talking about was long before. It was while we were still the only family we knew.)

My brother Leo, comedian, master of irony, isn't smiling. Maybe we don't have the same destination in mind, but the conversation has already begun and we let it lead us. Is he on his way to a job interview—the Post Office?—one of the many times my father has fired him from his diamond cutter's shop after a night searching for the stone that jumped off his cutting wheel and nestled somewhere in a crack between floorboards.

Our words turn into a scene between siblings that reminds me of a play I am reading, Eugene O'Neill's *Long Day's Journey into Night*.

"You don't know how good you have it." Leo says. We are past the bowling alley and the A & P, maybe on the way to the subway which is the spine of the city. It's why my parents picked this neighborhood, so my father could get to work easily without a car.

I look up at him, surprised, because even his tone is different. This isn't the brother who has always been so kind.

"What do you mean?"

"I mean you don't appreciate what you have. We were out on the street when I was your age."

"That was different. It was the Depression. Anyhow, we're not so rich now. My friends are richer."

"Do you hear yourself?" A pause to allow me to reflect. "You and your friends. They'll go to college and so will you."

"Maybe I won't. Maybe Daddy won't pay. I'll have to get a job, like you."

"You don't want to be like me. I worked for him from the time I was in high school."

"I work too. In the cleaning store after school."

"That's nothing. That's spending money, not making a living. You'll go to college. You get good grades. The teachers love you."

"Not all. I got a D in math and I can't do chemistry." I say it like I'm bragging.

"You'll go and you'll think it's your due."

Is he mad at me? I'm too stunned to cry. In fact, I can't figure out the right response. I think we just go our separate ways then, and he never takes up this theme again throughout the next sixty years. But it's how I know even Leo can be jealous.

Go Fish

BECAUSE SHE WAS FROM THE OLD COUNTRY. BECAUSE SHE WAS drawn to the gypsies. Because the Torah, religious law, was the Truth, and women only knew it second-hand in the Orthodox way. They mostly had to rely on lore, on word of mouth, to govern the household. So my mother was a devotee of superstition. And of course, anything bad that happened had an agent, even if it was only the jealous neighbors. No umbrella could be opened in our house, no hat thrown in haste on the bed. All the kashrut rules observed, well, religiously. Misused forks and knives, the ones designated for dairy that got accidentally stuck into meat, had to be buried overnight in the cleansing soil of the lawn. Fish were exempt. Fish were neutral although they breathed and bled like us, like chickens and cows did, but they were always kosher. Once, I remember a big, live carp swimming in the bathtub. Horribly, it would shortly be ground up and transformed like a fairy tale fish into gefilte fish for Passover. I couldn't eat it.

It was so easy to imagine a dialogue taking place between my mother and my brother Sidney to mark some reversal of fortune that would have been confided to him in Yiddish, their shared language:

Mother: Daddy was cutting a diamond and the stone flew off the wheel and got lost. I don't know what we'll do. A thousand dollars.
Sidney: There goes college.
Mother: That's set, you don't have to worry. But you know, I was thinking. Long ago, someone told me keeping fish in the house is bad luck. And here's your sister with those goldfish.

I like to believe that Sidney defended the fish, that he pled their innocence and told my mother it wasn't true. After all, he helped me set up the bowl and pick out pretty pebbles to put in the bottom. He taught me how to use the filter for their water. Carefully, with Sidney's help, I transferred the two chubby orange fish from the water-filled plastic bag they came in, a male and a female, I hoped, so there'd be babies, but who was to know? That first day, together we pinched food out of the packet and into the water for them. Still, magic would make a strong case with my mother. And wasn't it all over before she even told him?

I only know that one day I come home from school and my treasured goldfish are missing. They are entirely mine, almost the only thing in our house that is, my responsibility. I change their water each week. I put them in a pot while I rinse their bowl. I feed them in the morning, alone, sprinkle in a little fish food from the paper packet. It looks like sand. I've got a book from the pet shop that came with them to tell me what to do.

The bowl rests on the bureau in my room, close to the window so outside light can shine through. I adjust my eyes to follow the path of their swimming. I count the pebbles on the floor they will never stand on but that makes a grounding for their little lives. I love how sometimes the glass of the bowl makes them bigger, like a magnifying glass. I love them as if I could pet them. I'm proud I can take care of them. That something I do works, that they are thriving. Fish grow and grow, I have read in the book, depending on the size of the water you put them in. Someday I will have a pond in a backyard to keep them in and they will be twice their size.

"Where are the fish?" I ask my mother when I come downstairs, puzzled and a little apprehensive not to find them where I left them in the morning. "What happened to them?" My heart is beating fast. There's the start of a sinking feeling in my stomach. I can see in my mind a knock to the floor, spilled water, broken glass, fish fluttering. But I try to calm myself and say, hopefully, "Maybe you found someplace else to put them?"

Oh, if only. Piecemeal, I get it out of her. "You don't need them. What good are they? You can't play with them. They don't sit in your lap." She's trying to convince me of something. "It's a mess to clean around them. And they only bring bad luck." Then comes the embarrassed laugh she uses to hide bad news, even if she's sure she's right. "I had to get rid of them."

"You gave them away?"

"I flushed them down the toilet."

Sidney sighs and his slight giggle has a nervous edge. Is he trying to console me? "Anyhow, it's too late. There's nothing you can do. They're back in the ocean where they came from."

Sidney

If I get impatient—"Let me do it now!"—he might just walk away. So I hold it in. Sidney stands beside me. His mouth opens and closes in concentration. He's not aware of this. He loses himself and I do, copying him. He shapes the pieces of leather with a sharp knife from a template in the kit, gray-blue for wings, black, the head, yellow for its beak. He stirs the glue and shows me how to layer one shape over the next and press. We have the two frames and the cardboard backgrounds set out, waiting. We're at the dining room table, the only surface big enough to work on. Pads and newspapers protect the table; we're careful not to go deep or we could cut through to wood. We make two ducks. When the smelly glue dries, our mother will hang them flying toward one another on the wall of the screen porch where everyone who comes in through the front door will see.

Sidney is good with his hands. He has taken shop in school and knows how to fix, even build, things. He will grow up to be an engineer. Sometimes he helps me with projects for school. Once he tells me the Mafia is known as the Black Hand and I make a poster against evil with a filled-in shape of my hand in the middle. Another time, we glue gray thread to blue construction paper to stand for rain.

One day he is staining a bookcase my mother has bought and lets me help. The only place for books in the house before this is in the boys' room, a triangular shelf like a crooked arm under the bedside table they share. I come in uninvited when they're not home to read *The Amboy Dukes, Catcher in the Rye, Youngblood Hawke,* too grown up for me and so, irresistible.

But my mother has bought an unpainted bookcase, stores for such furniture have just come into being, and asked Sidney to "stain" it. This does not mean make a stain, something you don't want that won't come out no matter how hard you scrub, like the grape juice on my yellow blouse. No, this staining is on purpose. When we're finished it will stand against the wall of the living room, perpendicular to the couch, and it will go as far as the big, square opening to the dining room.

Sidney has spread out newspaper over the floor, you can't make anything without newspaper, and laid the bookcase on its side so he can work. The smell pricks my nose. I'm allowed to do a few strokes, then have to stand back and watch because he does it so much faster. He reminds me of Tom Sawyer, getting other children to pay him for a chance to paint the fence. I guess I would pay but I don't have to.

The color of the wood goes from pasty, knotted white to dark brown. It begins to look like furniture but never becomes that convincing, not as shiny as the wood claws on the feet of the couch. Is the bookcase meant for Sidney's schoolbooks? Prayer books? My mother's one novel, by Vera Caspary, that I one time read part of? Maybe it's to hold the encyclopedias she collects at the movies on Thursday, the way we got our silverware the year before, though she has forgotten to go some weeks, so there are big gaps in the volumes. No M or P, for instance. I do try to use them but the print is small and they often don't have whatever it is we are studying in school.

Still, the bookcase is a place for books, something that makes our living room complete, that's in everybody else's house.

A slide rule rests on Sidney's desk upstairs beside his loose-leaf. I'm curious, holding it when he comes into the front room to get back to work, and he's not mad. He shows me how it works although I never totally understand. I just like its movable parts; one layer slides over another, clicking like mahjong tiles.

It's white with its tiny lines and numbers. Longer than a ruler. Smooth like Turkish Taffy.

Sidney is free summers because he goes to school, high school and then junior college, and then real college, while I am still in elementary school. We have a lot of time together. He helps me develop photos I take with my matchbox-size camera I got with a cereal box top. Always something interesting, for instance, he tries to teach me chess though I prefer checkers. And we read books together.

One summer day we are sitting on the kitchen steps in the sun and Sidney is showing me a book he has bought at Leary's, the three-story used bookstore on Market Street he and Leo know. I don't go myself until I'm older but then I get to love it too, the smell of old paper and unvarnished wood floors. You could get lost in those corridors of books. He comes back with boys' books he buys for a few cents, books he didn't get to read when he was a child, like *Penrose and Sam*. The one he passes on to me this time is *Essays of Elia* by someone named Charles Lamb. It's an ancient book, the corners of the cover beaten down, torn. It's small and dark blue with funny print. He opens it to "A Dissertation Upon Roast Pig." That's a food I know is not kosher, and I feel a little funny reading about it.

The essay, I must have thought of it as a story because I didn't know what an essay was, tells how in China a boy who liked to set things on fire accidentally burned down the shed where the family's pigs were kept. He knew he was in trouble and tried to pull one of the dead pigs out in case maybe it was still alive. His fingers got burnt and he licked them.

I couldn't imagine how it tasted, but he liked it and pulled away one piece after another. In fact, he ate and ate until almost the whole pig was gone. When the boy's father came to beat him for playing with fire and ruining the shed, he convinced him to try a taste too. Word got out and they were arrested. It was apparently illegal to cook things before you ate them. But soon everybody all over China began to burn down their sheds to get roast pig to eat. It was only later they discovered they didn't have to burn down the shed but could just cook the pig. So Sidney introduced me to Charles Lamb and to satire and to the imagined deliciousness of forbidden food.

"I feel bad for the pigs," I told him and began to wonder, could roasted pork really taste that good?

"My Sidney, My Daddy"

IS THE TITLE OF MY NEPHEW NELSON'S DRAWING FROM WHEN HE was five, tacked up on the wall of my brother's nursing-home room. Under the words, the childish portrait, slanted eyes, circle face filled-in with pencil. Sidney's room is furnished like a monk's room, bed, chair, but also a flat black TV. My brother's children and grandchildren have brought me to visit. We take my brother out to a deli for lunch. It's food he likes and remembers, bagels, lox, eggs and onions. We borrow him from the Alzheimer's Unit, open plan, where doors do not lock and residents can move in and out of one another's rooms and a woman like a magpie comes into his room to steal his eyeglasses periodically. The only lock is on the outer door of the ward and no one inside can get past that. We borrow him from his dementia to which he will just as cheerfully return in a couple of hours. And the brother who teased me as a child is now a gracious paterfamilias with a shock of hippie-length white hair like Jerry Garcia, with pant legs his grown son rolls up for him, and so glad to see me, the last remaining member beside himself of his first family, the person in the world most like him.

Red Hair

THE FORTUNE-TELLER TOLD ME, "A MAN WITH RED HAIR AND money." And I did go out with a red-haired boy, but though his hair was brilliant, otherwise he held not much interest for me. He liked to say words backwards like *kumsch* for schmuck, and he believed in *padoodles*, that a car with a single headlight driving past was a signal to kiss and so grabbed me whether I was in the mood or not.

Red hair may be a sign of luck. Rita Hayworth, however, was born with black hair and a different name. Who would not want red hair? Trust me. Once I went as far as a drugstore rinse and felt for three months as though I wore a halo. The comfort red hair gives in the coolness of the world, that fire surrounding you, that choice. In childhood, I let a red-haired friend, Kitty—it ran in her family—for no reason I can remember, one winter day push me into a snowbank. Red hair is the color of honey, the color of freckles, the color of maple leaves or coal fires. People with red hair have a built-in nickname. They are called Brick, Rusty, Carrot Top, always an exaggeration.

Famous redheads of the past, if we are to believe paintings, are Christ, Judas as well, surprisingly, and Lady Godiva. Red hair is rare. Red hair is a pleasure to look at. It can help you pick someone out of a crowd. Of course, it can be a stigma if you're not beautiful. Then you are only funny looking, peculiar, though this too could be an asset. Woody Allen, self-named for the redheaded woodpecker, is an example. A gynecologist I went to, could his name have been Sater? told me during my examination it was obvious I was meant to be a redhead. Red hair is found everywhere in the world, though it is most prevalent in northern

Europe where the sun is not strong, especially in Ireland and Scotland, and among Ashkenazi Jews.

When I was 20 my black-haired brother, Sidney, brought home his new, red-haired wife. I saw the attraction. Together, they were like a game of checkers, a regal battle that continued for decades. Normally, she was shy and quiet, except for a sharp Jersey accent, but he incited the quick temper, the flushed cheeks latent to her coloring. She'd work as a drugstore cashier to give her children money for things he didn't approve of and encouraged them to eat what they wanted, cheeseburgers and cheesesteaks, even if it wasn't kosher, outside the house. I don't know when she ceased to be a natural redhead, maybe she never did, or the shade was artfully matched throughout her life.

When a redhead ages, I don't think she should settle for anything less. It's against nature. Last week in the skin doctor's office on my twice-yearly visit, because I, like real redheads, have extremely sensitive skin, a gray-haired woman smiled at me. I didn't recognize Mrs. Mackey, much envied red-headed neighbor of long ago, in a turban of gray hair, until the receptionist called out her name.

These days, on Saturdays at the cabin, I walk the fence beside a farmer's red-brown horse. They call him Red. He is more work- than racehorse even though his owner tries to ride him. He waits for me and keeps pace the length of his fence, shuffling and galloping as he's inclined. He wears a red harness over his blond mane. His tail is a plume of smoke the same shade. His teeth are square and even. He doesn't like to be petted on the white star of his long nose. His red-lashed eyes are friendly, and we commune by smell. I hold my gloved hand under the tear-shaped nostrils, twitching like tiny, windswept caves, and Red snuffles and snorts my scent.

Kitty

KITTY WAS THE BOSS OF ME FROM THE TIME WE MET, WHEN SHE pushed my face into a snowdrift as a kind of welcome to the neighborhood. We were the tallest girls in first grade, sitting together at the back of the classroom in our cotton dresses with puffed-up sleeves, and she lived only a dozen houses away. After school in warm weather, she'd call my name through the screen door and I came out to play with her on some patio mid-way between our houses, jacks and "A My Name." "A my name is Alice and I come from Alabama" was easy, it was like the song, and we knew what went with our own names, Kansas or Kentucky for her and England for me. I worried what would happen when we got to X and Z. I thought up Zena from Zebulon but we never got that far.

I was invited to help decorate Kitty's Christmas tree because we didn't have one. I loved Christmas and Easter; even my mother seemed to believe in Easter: parades and baby chicks (pathetically dyed pastel colors, who didn't live long) and new outfits. Once my mother had a blue serge Easter suit made for me at Blauner's. Kitty was Episcopalian and let me in on certain inside secrets. She told me Easter was when Christ died. "They hung him up on a cross?" Had she made it up? She could tell tales. She said the pretzel sticks in a canister at the store were called "prenzels" because they were shaped like pencils. When it was Christ's birthday we exchanged Evening in Paris cologne, Naked Maja soap, and stationery decorated with flowers, gifts we considered grown-up.

It was an old WASP neighborhood we lived in, populated with old WASPS who were dying off. When houses went up for sale, ethnics moved in, refugees who had survived the War as well as Jews like us from ghettos farther south in the city. That's how the city was changing. And after, Black families taking the same path. The new people were younger and had growing families. Kitty was the last white Protestant child on the block. She had to play with me or have no one.

Kitty always knew what was going on on our street, maybe because she went to the same church as some of the neighbors. She liked babies, so when a young mother moved in across from us, she had us go over and pay a call. They were from Texas, her husband was stationed at a nearby army base, and I liked to hear Cindy, the lady, talk. Not a lady exactly. I thought, maybe only a teenaged girl. I watched her fry steak in butter which I never knew you could. They rented; they wouldn't be staying long and didn't have much furniture or any lamps I could see. The house was so bright because they relied on ceiling fixtures, left on all the time. We got in the habit of going there. Once Cindy remarked that she had never met a Jew before. I said back, I never met anyone from Texas.

Cindy may not have wanted us around so much but she didn't seem to know anyone else. Once, she said, out of desperation, I guess, "Hey, you two, I need to go out to the store." With a long look back, she left us in the house alone with the doughy, blue-eyed infant. After a while we went into the room with the crib. The baby was bigger than any doll I had ever played with.

Just then he started to fuss. Kitty was brave. She went over and patted his stomach. I said, "Should we turn him over so he'll sleep?" I think I wanted to know what would happen if we did. She took the top and I took the bottom and we shifted him onto his side. He felt like a big sack of sugar but he did go back to sleep so we didn't disgrace ourselves when Cindy came home from the store, or maybe she had only gone to the park to sit for half an hour.

Kitty combed her hair in waves like Rita Hayworth. We both loved the movies and popular songs too, the ones on the radio and on the *Hit Parade* on TV. You could buy printed-out copies of the lyrics that we studied like we'd be tested on them. My arm thrown over her shoulder, the two of us bawled out, "I found my thrill on Blueberry Hill" as we walked in step up the street from my house to hers, her long, red hair streaming out like a flag.

Old

THERE WAS A TINY, ANCIENT WOMAN FROM THE NEXT BLOCK WHO came to us. My mother and others referred to her as the Old Lady and everyone knew who they meant. She moved like a bird, neck in and out, bobbing as it went forward. And as it rocked, side to side, for she did that too. She wore a flowered kerchief that fell forward over her forehead. The face beneath was brown and wrinkled like a paper bag used too many times. As she walked, she muttered incessantly, in rhythm to her steps, like someone praying. Yiddish was her language. My mother understood and liked to spend fifteen minutes, a half-hour with her, inviting her in, making tea. She felt sorry for her. She never doubted the Old Lady's strange stories. My mother translated as they spoke, for her own sake or mine. There would be a sharp intake of breath in almost every conversation: "My Gawd! The daughter she cared for her whole life threw her down the stairs!" My mother was angry and, I thought, looked at me a little suspiciously at that point, though I was not yet 10 years old. The Old Lady herself was small, no bigger than a child, and would have been easy to throw down the stairs, should anyone be mean enough to care to.

Survivor

I KNEW WHO HE WAS, KNEW HIM A LITTLE, AND HIS SMALL, PRETTY wife. They lived nearby. At least, I knew them both to say hello. A tall, broad-shouldered man in his forties, fifties, I was too young to tell. Light hair and bluest eyes. I'm not sure of his name and would I have called him Rudy, if that was it, or Mr. something? They were Displaced Persons who had managed to get out of the War alive.

That summer day I lay on the screen porch, reading one of my long Russian novels. I read them all day while there wasn't school, often into the night. It was hot. I was wearing only a halter and shorts. No one else was home, and I lay so long, sweating, scarcely moving except to turn a page. I was startled to hear the doorbell and to see the outline of a man. To be brought back to myself, where I lay, feeling suddenly exposed.

The way I read, it was as if I, myself, were no longer present. My feelings merged with the characters so that I was in a state of languor and total compliance. What they felt, I felt. I was a product, like them, of the plot's machinations, the coolness and distance of someone else's words. It tore me away from the day and what was foremost in my own mind. I couldn't think with my usual self-consciousness of how I appeared to the world, even my family. That's how I read, with my whole soul.

Then to be brought back to my usual teenage awkwardness, almost naked, my hair a mess, seeing myself through someone else's eyes. It was hard to pull away from Natasha and a war I didn't even know the name of. I felt spied on almost, only the screen door between me and outside. And when the man spoke, it was out of the foreignness of another language. He might have been someone in my book with an unpronounceable last name. And of course, he made me think of his own war, the one he had come to us out of.

So mindful, I was, that I shouldn't let a strange man in while I was at home alone. All I could do was go to the door and explain that my parents weren't here, they were the ones to take care of it, whatever it was. "Just tell them I stopped by," he said, with some embarrassment. And I did tell them. I knew my mother would want to go to their house, to chat and find out why he had come but that my father would discourage her.

Maybe his was just a neighborly visit to say hello and introduce himself. To become better acquainted or see if my father could give him a job. But on our street we stayed boxed into our small, connecting houses that were only big enough for ourselves. The street was where we exchanged words, neutral territory.

I didn't see Rudy again even to say hello. Instead it came down to us through the chain of houses that he had died. They thought he had taken his own life. And was I in some way responsible? I felt ashamed to have turned him away. Imagine, I thought, to survive the Nazis, but not us and our neighborhood.

Neighborhood

I OBSERVE THE NEIGHBORS MAINLY IN THE COMMON CORRIDOR OF the street. At some point they must all come out from the square houses that touch uncomfortably. The one or two single mothers with children we feel sorry for, we don't know what has become of the fathers. The neighbor who owns the house next to Cindy, Mr. Dwyer, a tall, straight-shouldered man with white hair, a policeman. Sometimes we see him in uniform and it reassures us. His two daughters, one, bright-haired and beautiful, and the other kind, plain, devout.

The neighbors. Yet they are not monolithic. Whenever do they act together as a body? Maybe only in their silent pact of approval or disapproval. "What will the neighbors think?" my mother says. And I know it is a governing principle of our lives.

Suddenly, a Black family moves in on the next block. The word is that a church has bought the property and brought them in, or that maybe Communists have. This is the McCarthy era, after all, and much is attributed to Communists. But the neighbors have dug in and are not yet ready for white flight. One small family, one house. Yet within a week that house is fire-bombed and you can walk up and witness the empty dark shell of a house that was once so much like our own.

In grade 4A, and 4A only, we have in our class an African-American boy named Jefferson. His mother has pulled him out of a ghetto school and enrolled him in our school because it is safer and cleaner, because she hopes he will get a better education. He is painfully shy. He could be made of stone. We say we don't want to make him self-conscious, so he is ignored for his own sake. Oh, the heartbreaking respect he shows, appearing each day in a white shirt and tie. He sits next to me in the last seat of the fourth row, I am on the third. One day the teacher takes me aside and asks if I can bring him home with me until his mother, who, like our Eveline, works as a maid in the neighborhood, can pick him up, and I say yes. I'm curious what he thinks of us, what he's like. It turns out he's nice, and funny. He notices what goes on in class, even if he doesn't say a word, even if, like me, he never raises his hand and has to be called on by the teacher. He tells me who he thinks is a baby, who is a weasel. Who he has seen cheat on tests. We laugh together and play checkers. I'm glad he feels so at ease with me.

My mother brings us fudge-striped cookies and milk and his "Thank you, Ma'am" impresses her, I can tell. But although she has made him feel welcome, after he is picked up, looking at me with sad eyes she tells me, "You can't bring him here again." She's worried: "What will the neighbors think?"

Feather

"A HUNDRED AND SIXTY-EIGHT POUNDS. THAT'S 48 MORE THAN you should weigh. You could be carrying a seven-year-old around on your back."

Ashamed, I take as an insult what the school nurse says. But there might as well be another child I carry inside. I stuff him with sweets and every good thing I want to eat. He's on my back and his legs hold on and cross over my belly. He won't let go. I wish I could drop him in a river.

I talk my mother into summer camp that year. For weeks we sew labels that I letter with my name in India ink into white tee shirts and shorts. Do they think I'll forget who I am? Rebecca up the street is going. At camp, everyone is crazy about her, her curled hair, her tiny waist. She lasts just four days. So then I have no one to talk to except the girl in the next bunk, Lois, and I'm happy to be her friend. Lois has freckles, something I always wanted. And she is built straight up and down, thin as a plank, sideways. She doesn't take up a lot of space, as I do.

"Look up there," I tell her one night, pointing to the mice crossing the bunkroom on the eaves overhead, and she's properly scared so I don't have to be the only one. "Oh, God," she says, "what if they get dizzy and fall down?" We go together with flashlights to the smelly lavatory. You have to have a buddy to go anywhere, even into the swimming pool. She is my buddy, at least until Janet comes.

We all eat together in a big wooden house. One day the cook has put so much salt in the oatmeal it tastes like sea water. When I say so and don't want to eat it, the counselor persuades me to take seven spoonsful. That's how I go about everything here. I try,

I really do, and then turn away when I can't do more than that.

If I'm lonely and scarcely say a word to anyone for a whole month, it doesn't matter so much. Everything is different here. The green fields and the trees, the world that smells fresh and bitter when I wake up. I didn't know morning was so early, damp and cool, that drops of water would cling to high grass and get your sneakers wet. That you could go for hours without a meal or even a snack.

Fridays, there's the campfire. After we toast marshmallows and sing songs, prizes are given out, feathers to the bravest warriors (campers). I never know anyone who wins. Then once I think I hear my name called. Did I maybe do something wrong? Awkwardly, I make my way to in front of the fire while someone beats an Indian drum. I stand before the camp director, the "Chief," who holds out to me the special feather for Perseverance, which I didn't even know was brave.

a ciggy, be seen. At the wide tables, put next to someone you'd want to be up against. Instead, you stand out here, exposed. All eyes on you, flayed by eyes. Wind puffing up the barrel shape of your skirt. This once, could it be different? Feverish, mysterious, "You belong to my heart, and a million guitars are still playing." Song in your head, the almost possible torrid radio night song that will later carry you into sleep.

Car

A dream is all times and in it, I am everyone and everything.
My car and I, made up of gas and dust like a star. My car is up
on wooden blocks. It's just a skeletal car and I don't know how
to drive, but I am sitting in the driver's seat. There is no bottom
to my car. I look down to see the ground. I run my car, pedal it
like a tricycle. I run it like mad. I go forward, I go back. I park,
hooking my arm over a seatback. By means of its own hydraulics,
my car is lowered onto the road. By then it's dusk. The road is
clogged with the conniving animals of traffic. SUVs gloat from
their superior vantage. Low slung, slouching sports cars slip
in where they can, shiny black and red. High wheelers belch
foul smoke. In some cars, tinted windows are closed against the
stench and disguise whoever is inside, maybe some mob boss.
In most cars the air conditioning creates its own atmosphere.
Once, a woman's hand extends from the driver's side, pale with
a trifling of gold rings, gracefully undulating to unheard music.
I drive, I pass, I stop, rubble and retreads lining the way. I run a
third lane gamut of iron bars. Spokes poke up from below, allow
me to pass, like a series of tilted turnstiles.

Is he trying to protect me? And from what—Danger? Heartbreak? But then I have to remember Philadelphia as it was in 1955. We'd be the only mixed-race couple on the street. Even in Center City, people looked at us with surprise or contempt or turned their gaze away. In that "daring" movie of its time, *Island in the Sun*, Harry Belafonte is in love with Joan Fontaine but they don't even once dare kiss.

I WANT THAT MOMENT
TO COME AGAIN

Previous page: Leo at work.

Spartans

It's Leo who finds that name in a history book. The others like it and agree. They are a team and it means athletes, warriors, people trained to endure. They look around at empty lots, broom handles, halves of balls. They like what they see. All afternoon grass dances away from garter snakes and the ground balls they call hits. My brother seems not to mind that little by little his precious baseball cards are being fed to the furnace, getting it started. Double pneumonia leaves a spot on his lungs in that cold, rented row house. I picture an *x*, like a signature.

Eldest of us, he is first to drive or be drunk, first, as noted, to run away from our mother's warm tremolo in the kitchen after dark.

It's WWII and at school, at home, he's a student of war and hardship. He fills scrapbooks with cartoons of Hirohito and photos of bombings from the newspaper, volcanoes of black and white dots. I watch him pull out strands of tinfoil or whatever else is left shining in our lives and roll them into a bright colossal ball.

The Spartans, it says in white script on the backs of red baseball jackets they have made for them in high school. All their lives when they meet, they are slapping each other in the gut, stretching up to reach imagined baskets, crouching in the hunched wait of infielders. On the name, no one could fault them. What life is there beyond the body? What history?

Homing

THE PARROT SLEEPS WITH HIS HEAD UNDER HIS WING. THE PEO-
ple nod off, chin to chest. I find my brother in the little enclave
of wheelchairs in the home where he now lives, permanent New
Jersey. His baseball cap, "My name is Leo," stuck on his head
backwards. A woman beside him grabs my arm before I can get
to him. "Help me, help me!" she cries out, making the motions
of pulling off her sweater. The nurse sees me and asks, "Are you
here to see Jean?" I shake my head but I have to help. When Jean
is out of the sweater, she starts to moan, "Where's my sweater?
Someone took my sweater!"

"What did you have for lunch?" I ask my brother. "That's a
good question," he replies, with a roll of his eyes, to let me know
he doesn't have the answer and finds this a little funny. It's like
what mist does, coming between where you are and where you
are going. He would like to get out of here. He doesn't know that
he won't. Likewise, he would like to get out of his confusion, as
if it were a place. Sometimes he imagines it is a tour he is on, an
interminable vacation. "The people are nice. We always have
good weather." Can he bear it, this wrenching from his house
and the life that he knows, the porch under its awning, the kitch-
en table, the big TV, and not far, the boardwalk where he could
sit, inhaling sea air, "What a pleasure!"?

The course of the disease is said to be seven years, like some-
thing biblical, like a curse. When it began he told me, "I want
you to know you were a good sister." In case he forgot who I
was, our shared past. My mother did her duty and my father did.
Leo saw what was missing and tried to fill in. He installed a new
furnace, a first refrigerator. More, what he brought to our house

was a sense of ease, of fun. And for me, every good thing I owned: the plastic radio that sang me to sleep at night, a red imitation alligator overnight case for sleepovers, an Olivetti typewriter. The TV where we watched Dean Martin and Jerry Lewis cavort in tuxes, Jerry jumping up into Dean's arms like a dysfunctional child. As I would jump up into Leo's arms if I were still small enough. We were crazy for the jokes, the wild dancing. The two of us, laughing, pals. And I see it's still in place, that braying laugh of his, all the air sucked in. I think how he loved to wear a tux at formal parties, on shipboard. So handsome. That video of his son's wedding, at the end all the parents and their friends, crooning, close and sentimental.

Now, here, he tries to do what he's told, like a good child. But he hasn't lost his sense of humor. When the doctor asks, "And what did you do for a living, Mr. G?" he answers, "I used to be an exotic dancer," and the doctor looks unsure. Does he recognize how funny my brother is, or does he put it down to the disease? Leo is very popular here, like an entertainer. One of the high school volunteers, goes by, waving. He sees my brother mumbling to himself. "That's Leo," he says, "always telling his stories." And he is. Birney schoolyard. The six types of ball they played. Stick ball, half ball, softball, handball, kickball, basketball. The Spartans, his friends and teammates, "since we were six years old," and he holds his hand out flat at the height of his thigh.

"They came, I think it was last week." (Is he making this up? But later it's confirmed by my sister-in-law.) I ask about work, the shop he inherited from my father and kept going for fifty years. Was Leo ever afraid there? "Why would I be afraid?" I think he must never have been afraid in his life. Anyhow, he didn't keep diamonds in his pocket, except to make a delivery a couple of doors away. He trusted insurance and safes. Mostly, he trusted people. That acute but quiet humor, cracks he made with a straight face or eyebrow raised in irony. No one on Sansom Street better liked.

For so long he was the sole diamond cutter in the city, subject of a newspaper story with photos. "You put the diamond on the wheel." He makes the motions. "You flatten each facet. A diamond has 48 facets," he looks over to me as he explains. What I don't ask about, can't take part in, the conversation he is always having inside himself.

I turn his wheelchair and my wicker visitor's chair to the glassed-in wall of birds. Parakeets, maybe they're called budgies. Green, blue, brown, and white. Dull and bright. Miniature and free, flitting among the dozen little baskets that serve as nests. Attaching claws to a swinging bar that hangs from the ceiling. Alike in their differences. The parrot cage gets pulled away at night but these small birds are allowed to remain. They carry straw in their beaks to go through the motions of building, building. But the nests are pre-constructed modules. A female poses at the opening but flies down to the pebbled floor and returns to another dwelling, waits for a different mate. Then singly, or several at a time, they dip to the tray of birdseed and water, rise to the waving swing. My brother asks to be turned around.

Like the birds, he's the spirit of himself without the trappings of a life. Without a house or furniture. Removed from everything, even what he formerly could reach with the probing of memory. But there are ties, there are word clues to what he is thinking. And he'll say he's sorry when he's been borrowed from the actual conversation I am attempting.

He tries to please. He's like a houseplant slanting toward the last remembered source of light. But he doesn't think, he says, this place is doing him much good, he should get out soon. I find an abandoned newspaper, turn to the comic/puzzle page. Why haven't I thought of this before? We will be on the same page. Sudoku. I don't know how to do it. I read out the rules, the numbers. My brother remembers his arithmetic. "Five and seven are twelve." "Nine and six are fifteen." Yes, yes, that's true, but what we have to do here is put them in a line, or a box, not add them up. I hate to negate what he is doing, he's getting the right answers, just to the wrong questions. But soon his head has dropped to his chest and his eyes close. I see I've lost him. He returns though and we sit like this, half in, half out of someone else's parameters, trying to do something neither of us has the wit for.

When I look and he has no front teeth, I am afraid for a moment he has swallowed them chewing on the chocolate peanuts I brought. I have forgotten, as has he, the cup of water where the dental bridge floats, magnified, on his bedside table. He smiles to show me the empty space, like a Halloween pumpkin.

Just Dreaming

*In my dream, Father Death is waiting and looks a lot like Keith
Richards, lead guitar for the Rolling Stones. Leo takes my hand
and I place my other hand on my heart a minute where the pain
is. Then he walks me towards Sansom Street in his brown leather
house slippers. He's about 50, the age when he was most hand-
some, when the* Bulletin *did the profile of him with pictures;
in one there's a jeweler's loupe in his eye. Together we pass the
carved art-deco facades, the flickering gemstones nestled on red
velvet pillows that sit at the base of high, gilded windows. When
we enter 726, the self-elevator, a cage, a claustrophobe's night-
mare, jumps and starts, makes it up to the third floor, and we are
at the greasy gate of the small dark shop where Leo and our fa-
ther, later Leo and his son, have sat on cramped benches behind
the slick wheels where diamonds turned. In a corner, the set of
scales, wood and steel behind glass, delicate enough to calibrate
the carats of diamonds, waits like a sailing ship in a bottle.*

Under the Sign of Leo

WHEN IN JUNIOR HIGH I HEAR ABOUT ASTROLOGY, THAT PEOPLE believe you are born under the sign of rotating stars that guide you, I am not surprised to learn that Leo the Lion is my sign. In my family, my brother Leo is the oldest and most worldly, the bravest it seems of any of us. From the beginning he looks out for me. While I'm a toddler, he brings me nursery books, my first books. I remember a picture of a baby in a cradle dangling from a treetop, and the rhyme beneath it, "Rockabye, Baby." I'm convinced it's a girl baby like me. Why is she not frightened at her predicament? I surely was.

The constellation Leo, governing part of July, part of August, it turns out, is a fire sign like the hot summer, bright and showy. It's said there's no keeping a Leo back. They are fearless, competitive. They want to come out ahead. But when I'm grown I admit my birth date to a friend who knows how shy I am. We laugh about it and decide that maybe because I was born on the cusp and had those aspirations but wasn't likely to act on them, I was a closet Leo.

Looking back, that seems fair to say. From first grade on, I never raised my hand, even to go to the bathroom. When I was asked to come forward, I instinctively stepped back, except only once I can think of. The teacher had brought a cow's heart to school and a sharp knife. I was willing to conduct the experiment, cut through the heart and show the class its four chambers, like little white-walled rooms, but only because no one else in third grade wanted to. Miss Ritchie said I might grow up to be a famous surgeon but I demurred. I had learned early to disqualify

137

myself. In a circle game if I was singled out, it was just to be "it," target of the ball, unable to outrun it.

I would never be class president. Once, vice president, once, managing editor of the high school paper, not editor-in-chief. If someone offered me a prize or a hot job over my lifetime, I would likely say no. But I liked, from an early age, to compete with myself. I chewed bubble gum and practiced so I could blow bubbles in an ever-greater circumference, and in trials with other kids, I'd win. When the bubble burst over my face and had to be cut out of my long braids, that was all right, that was the price of excellence. And later, I developed skill at the bat'n'ball, a contraption that cost 25 cents. I begged for it once when we were in the 5 & Dime. I held it flat out and bounced the ball at the end of the rubber band to a count of five hundred, and if I outbatted any kid on the block, it was a contest with myself that I won.

And I was checker champion for a season at the playground in Atlantic City where we sat under a tent squishing pebbly dirt between our toes. The hot wind blew and the air stung with sand. I won against all challengers, but that was because I was fat and unathletic, an indoor type, and had perfected my skill with the help of my brothers, who always beat me. I liked being inimical, as I had imagined my cousin Esther, who I was supposed to be named for. I longed to be set apart though I didn't want to seem "in the game." Maybe that's not the right way to say it. I'd be willing to seem in it as long as I didn't let it go to my head.

For the most part, a curtain closed off ambition, possibility. I came to see that Now, the present moment, was not fixed. It moved toward you and as suddenly, away. You'd wait stolidly, aware finally only of its passing. You were liable to be hit by it, knocking you off your feet. In retrospect, I'm sorry. In retrospect I want that moment to come again when the program director invites me to California or the famous architect suggests dinner and a night on the town in Rome.

But I had my reasons, fear that I could not sustain admiration. That by nature, I would have to reveal my inadequacy. For much of my life it was not possible for me to speak in public, even in the intimacy of a car with one other person that I might have loved.

World's Most Timid Person

I GOT UP ON A HORSE (ONCE). I GOT UP ON SKATES, ON A BIKE, AND fell and fell. I even got down into a boat and trusted it. Swam into deep water but with such trepidation. I got through a crowd, got to the front of the room. Always, though, I tried not to be first. I got naked, entered a bed under sheets with someone else. And more than once. All of it was hard, at least at first. Wasn't it? Like my parents, brave in their lives, yet timid in the world. I learned from my mother to fit sideways in pictures. And she taught me to iron a shirt, back to front because a man wanted to make a nice appearance. I learned to enter the tip of the iron into the points of collars, into all the intricate crevices, as if the shirt were the flattened insides of an ear. And I saw how all of us in our house were yoked to the outside, moving in the expected rotation of the world, blind to it all, but continuing.

THE WALLS SEEM TO HAVE
SLID FORWARD

Previous page: Everyone else and Nany.

Gold Ocean

*The entire ocean, it seemed to me then, was golden. It might
have been the time of day, sunrise or sunset. Or for assonance,
ol- and oce-, o, the mouth stuck in an open position like the sea.
No matter, it came up under the boardwalk in white frills and
the woman's heavy arm rose through it and signaled over her
head, her shoulder falling back into the waves like the wheeling
of dolphins. Even from the back I knew this was the heavy swim-
stroke of my mother. Of course, I wanted to join her but couldn't
find the beach, the way in. My companions, the young couple
from the bus and a little girl who materialized out of nowhere,
were all searching the island too for the front of that orange-y
ocean.*

    *This is how it came to be. The others were strangers to me.
We'd met at the rear of the crowded bus where we stood close
together. The girl, the older one, where did the little one come
from? had long red hair in a ponytail so she was called Rusty.
Her companion, really he was her follower, was dark-haired
and uncoordinated. She held a bouquet of tea roses against her,
breathing in the scent, but the bouquet of eels was his. It was
slippery and he dropped it. She was getting off at the back door
and motioned with a toss of her too-bright hair. She clicked her
tongue, disgusted, waiting for him to pick up the cone of fallen
eels and follow. Her gestures affirmed that really it was of no
interest to her what he did. Meanwhile, I spotted someone whose
home-permed gray hair reminded me of women in the neighbor-
hood in the 1950s.*

    *She might have been the lady next door or maybe not. She
lay stretched out on the straw seats at the front reserved for senior*

citizens. She wasn't well and her doctor was patting the back of her flowered housedress. Soon, though, she managed to rise and stood with us at the back door. Her posture was surprisingly straight and youthful. She seemed in perfect form but for the splash of blood between her shoulders. Then the bus door opened and the young couple with the two bouquets descended. I followed in their wake as the bus made a little curtsying motion and the old woman got off and disappeared, she might have been swallowed up by the sidewalk, and the little girl too. We others were hurrying over a rough, herringbone pattern of boardwalk. Below, the nervous gold ocean scattered its apron of white foam, fanning out and retreating, and we went along it looking for an opening.

Maybe it took two or three anxious evenings. I know I didn't get him on the first try, but eventually I did. We took him to the vet to be rehabilitated and fed him to bursting to make up for his ordeal, though we ourselves, as I've said, were not eating much. When I went to the store, I ordered long, thin, finger-style rolls and 100 grams of cheese or prosciutto, "Un etto," 100 grams, I'd say, and even if that wasn't right, the shopkeeper understood. And weekly I stopped at the butcher's with the open shopfront and the gaping canvas awning where I splurged on scallops of veal for veal marsala or scaloppini. In my tiny kitchen, if I wasn't quick enough pounding and flouring, Smith, grounded, took off with one or more scallops in his mouth behind my back. "Sera, Signora," the butcher greeted me as I passed, but I couldn't really converse. My Italian was confined to buying food.

Tivoli

MAYBE BECAUSE THE SIGN I WAS BORN UNDER WAS A FIRE SIGN, I have always paid special attention to water. Could I have approached Tivoli, that park close to Rome, those balletic fountains, unaware of the watery chasm, the ocean I had passed only months before? Mindful of it for sure that day, sun glancing off the erupting waters. The people beside us, are they speaking Italian or English? A pretty woman in a beige polka-dotted summer dress with a white belt and open-toed sandals. The tall man beside her, his wide, expressive mouth bracketed by a heavy black mustache. Perhaps he has grown it for her because he is learning what will please her. The water dazzles and dizzies me. It's the heat or the beautiful lunch in town, roast chicken in a piquant sauce, too heavy for the time of day, or maybe that is the day we ate at a country villa, where lights were strung along the outdoor tables, the little bright-colored chicken rushing past, unknown to us, destined to be our dinner? Each of us stands now before a fountain, before a particular jet of water as if it has a personal utilitarian function, to soothe or to provide ablution. The fountain I have annexed I am reluctant to relinquish. I stand, wait, as it performs for me alone, air between it and me filled with light translucent as lemon peel in sunlight. Welcome to water in all its bright guises, nymph or little god. Faint with light, at last I retreat. I find a door to an inside and now, enclosed by terra cotta walls, adjust to ancient coolness and dark. An emperor's tomb. An uneven, sandy floor, and I stumble against the carved sarcophagus, box of stone. I cannot see my feet, the darkness dimming the present to imagination. Light leaks in from outside, squeezing through the partially open doorway. I feel the heat on my skin, shiver, I can hardly breathe, sweating and chilled at once, having already lost myself to myself, now, here, part of time.

The Crossing

It is spring. I have come cross-Atlantic in a black wool dress, my only black dress. It is a sheath with a skirt that flares at the knee. I have worn it dancing the tango clumsily with an Argentinian dental student at the University. I have worn it whenever a black dress is called for.

This is how it begins. I am on the terrace of the Rome apartment, sitting in the sunshine, the heat withheld, it's only morning. Someone is at the door. No one ever knocks, who do we know here? And the visitor is only a deliveryman with a telegram from my sister-in-law Bobbi, "COME HOME IMMEDIATELY." Nothing else. I know, of course, someone has died. It can't be Daddy. That would mean I'd never be able to forgive myself for leaving. Then I must will it to be my mother. I imagine a future for my father, learning to eat alone, to cook, to walk up to the A & P, even five more blocks to Penn Fruit, to wheel the shopping cart home with his small needs. How neat he will keep himself, the house. I see him for the first time washing dishes.

I can't telephone from our apartment (no phone). I know the consulate will put through a trans-Atlantic call and we go there. The consul, or whoever it is I see seated before an American flag, is a restrained middle-aged man in a suit. I wait until the connection is made and Bobbi is telling me, "He had a heart attack. Middle of the night. The paramedics came." Each word is a jab I feel in my own heart. Whenever one of us left to marry, my father had a heart attack, maybe to mark the loss. "They couldn't revive him."

The man behind the desk doesn't know what I want from him, and he isn't able to give much beyond accommodation and a formal sympathy. We go back to our apartment in a block of flats in a staid Roman neighborhood and I put on the black dress and manage to get to Fiumicino airport. I haven't slept for 24 hours. My eyes close for maybe a minute. I wake in my window seat, at least I think I'm awake, to find my father keeping pace, walking alongside the plane. He's on the wing or treading air, looking as I first knew him, his face, handsome, unlined. He's smiling, reassuring me. He's there for me alone.

There's a switchover in Milan, the only flight I can get at the last minute, and I take a taxi. I stop crying long enough to tell the driver where I'm going, why I'm crying. I try to say it in Italian but he speaks a little English. "Let me take you someplace first." I don't want him to, I don't want to go anywhere else, I tell him. Why does he think I am a tourist? I won't see anything through my tears. But he won't be discouraged. When we get to the giant cathedral, the Duomo, he stops and holds the taxi door open. I don't tell him I'm not Catholic. I go up the steps and enter the giant doorway into a cave-like darkness. And I see this is what I want, after all, to withdraw from the dazzling sunlight. I want to be told what to do, to be taken care of. How small I feel in the scale of this grandeur. Gradually, I become aware of the flickering candles, the glint of the red glasses that hold them, most of all, of the light filtering down like gold dust from above. In niches against the walls, I make out the pale, shimmering colors of saints' robes. I walk forward toward the altar, to the statue of the dead man.

Mother Sitting

THE NARROW HALL FROM THE KITCHEN TO THE DINING ROOM is a bottleneck, a little like the birth canal, you felt, because it was where you left your mother and your finished breakfast and, passing the open door to the cellar steps where anything could be waiting, went out into the rest of the house, the rest of the world, school, for instance, or wherever you had to go.

But today, you go the other way. Your mother is still in the dark blue dress, the color of her wedding dress, which she has worn to sit *shiva*, the period of mourning for a loved one, even though the black cloths that draped the mirrors are gone. Her lips have the thin veneer of lipstick almost worn off. The house never gets much light and the kitchen seems aglow as you pass through the dim screen porch, the French doors to the living room, the open, vanished partition leading to the barely used dining room.

The walls seem to have slid forward, the whole house smaller than you remember. Then that narrow passage to the kitchen where Mom sits on one of the white, painted chairs pulled up to the flowered oilcloth of the table. When you first went to school, after what felt like a lifetime of waiting, she became Mom, no longer Mommy. You never said Dad, though—even now when he is gone, he is Daddy.

If my mother is waiting for him to return, as she used to, the day will never end for her. She won't know what to do.

"What will I do?" she asks. There is no precedent for going on without him, even for eating or preparing a meal for herself. This house, the scene of so many battles and misunderstandings between you two. Where you were drummed out of the religion by her and the rabbi's wife. Where your wedding meant the end of your welcome here.

"I know what you must feel. I do. I have a husband now. I know what it would be to lose him." Will she say something wounding in response? It's what you expect, still raw from the recent past. But "You're just kids," she says. "You're just married. I lived with your father 40 years."

In the shopping bag you carry is veal from the closest kosher butcher. There's a frozen vegetable in the fridge. You have never been encouraged to cook in this kitchen but now she will not put up a fight. You are heady with European cuisine, you've read Julia Child and gone to restaurants. Tonight, you will try to make veal scaloppini. But the only wine in the house is what you find in the pantry, reserved for Passover. So you gamely open the jug of Manischewitz and cook with it and pour a little for both of you to drink.

You have put your battered suitcase, your father's varnished straw suitcase which he took once to Europe on a diamond-buying trip, upstairs on the bed of your childhood room. How narrow and monastic it feels, the single bed you were so happy to have at six, when the family moved to a bigger house and you no longer had to sleep with your mother.

Your brother Sidney would like you to stay forever, isn't it a daughter's duty? To leave your husband and move back to take care of your mother. She is so vulnerable and receptive, so unthreatening at this moment. You will stay, but not forever.

Only one other time does my mother seem so much to need me. Six years later, when she is a permanent resident of the Home for the Jewish Aged, specifically, the dementia ward. There is plaque in her brain, her doctor tells me.

I will see later a blurry shot in the *Jewish Exponent* of my mother here, dancing with a nurse, "One two, three," it says in the headline. And it's thrilling and a little amazing that she can still dance, she had so loved to when she was young. I have prepared myself for how I will find her, different from before, from how she was in the house where we lived together, everything wrong here, as if she had been accidentally misplaced.

This once when I come, as it turns out, even more so. I arrive and am mysteriously turned away. She is not there and my heart jumps. Is she gone? Then I learn that she has been sent to Einstein, the hospital nearby, for a "minor urological procedure." They don't tell me what it is and I wouldn't know probably any more than she would. I walk through city blocks to the hilly hospital grounds I rolled down and sledded on not so many years before. I take the elevator up to a surgical floor. I'm a little nervous about being here alone, about what might transpire, whether I will be wanted, whether she will even know me. But today I have my mother to myself, no other Alzheimer's patients, no hovering nurses, and no older brothers who have a greater claim, their visits more frequent and their connection to her stronger. I envy her recognition of them though I later learn she calls both Sidney; she knows at least that they are family. When we are all together, I am the stranger, an observer, on the sidelines of this little group—in the way, I feel.

The room is small, pale green, but not as antiseptic as I had feared. Her bed has rails, no need for the cloth restraints that anchor her to her wheelchair in the nursing home, so this time I'm spared seeing her tethered like an animal. She wears a printed hospital gown that ties in front; how thin my stout mother has become. Her gray hair, tending to wildness like mine, except when it was washed and shiny Friday nights before she lighted candles, now a smooth and luminous silver. I'm struck by how beautiful she is, empty of anxiety like this.

But then suddenly, she blinks and starts. Her green eyes, not so vacant as I've seen them, dart with terror. I pull up the visitor's chair and take her hands that are manic and thrashing, to still them. She moans and makes little wordless cries formed of pain or fear. She looks at me and tries to speak, but who knows what she remembers of words, whether they are just sound without meaning, whether she croons them to soothe herself.

She hasn't had the operation yet. She has never, in fact, been in a hospital except to give birth. I try to reassure her the way you would a child. I remember the care that showed on her face as she looked down at me while I was in bed with croup or chicken pox. The lollipops, pastel colored, that she specially bought because I liked them, to ease my sore throat. Her hand or her lips on my forehead to check for fever. It's the only part of me she touches.

"It's all right. I'm here," I tell her. "They need to do some little thing. It will make you feel better." I'm hoping this is true. After a while she calms. She doesn't pull her hands away from mine but leans into me, wanting to trust, allowing herself to be comforted.

Philadelphia

MY CITY, WHERE I WAS BORN, HAVE ALWAYS LIVED. I AM SITUATED now in the center, Center City, it's called. Like the river that is stuck in the middle and can't get out. The city is built on a grid; I'm never lost, even in the most remote parts. The central street is Broad, which it is, wide enough for six lanes of traffic. It should be 14th Street because the one just before is 13th and the one after is 15th. Quip of an old boyfriend, I remember he played the banjo, "Maybe Broad is the Native American word for 14th." Once we held each other on an old couch all night. The whole time I knew him, I could hardly think of anything to say, mute tongue of a lizard flicking out with not a word to claim him.

In high school once I sat with classmates in Rittenhouse Square. We had come for a lecture at the Alliance Française to get extra credit in French class. I remember I pointed to the skyscrapers surrounding us. "Someday I'll live in one of those," I bragged, but I never did. My first apartment was over a furrier's. The pelts of dead animals hung in the back. The two departing roommates who shared, I knew from my summer secretarial course. "Why are you moving?" I asked, and then, embarrassed, made a joke of it, "There aren't roaches, or anything, are there?" They looked at each other and stared me down. But of course there were.

Walking the streets that I already loved, past stores, art galleries, restaurants, I'd take note of some older woman, recognizing her, maybe she was famous, an artist, long, black hair and straight back, her waving scarves or poncho, clothes I wished I could wear. I'd read about her or seen an exhibit of her sculptures of the unlit space behind a shelf or between the legs of a chair, shapes of emptiness. Or a musician, a violinist, one of the few women in the orchestra while I was young. Or someone famous to me, a teacher I might once have had, marking her in my mind, watching her age over the years, over the rest of her life, hair graying, torso widening, morphing through all her various forms, pretty to utilitarian. I wonder if likewise, someone now is keeping track of me.

Today

I AM THINKING: OF THE SLEEPING MAN ON THE BUS I SIT DOWN beside. He might have been drunk but as easily only tired, reeling from hard work. A baseball cap is slid forward over his eyes and his tee shirt shows under a work jacket. He jerks up his head and hurries to the exit two stops after I get on. As he reaches the front I notice the carrier bag where his feet were and its contents, butcher-papered parcel and something like a sandwich in white paper. "Mister! Mister!" I call out but he is still sleeping as he exits and hurries down the street, even if his eyes are open, and he doesn't hear the woman who raps on the window to get his attention with her cane. I am weighed down with my own purchases. It is pouring out. I have no umbrella or would I have grabbed his bag and run after him down the crowded street, crying "Mister! Mister!"?

That night while it is still raining, I hear a knock at the door of our house on a tiny, quiet city street. Odd, especially as Lee, my husband, has installed a new lit doorbell to replace the dimmed-out old one, in the belief that delivery people will see it after dark, they come as late as 8, and not knock as someone is doing, which we rarely hear over the TV or because we are on another floor. The house is a century old and held together by Lee's clever patches and modifications.

I did hear it, the knock, I just never like to answer the door when I'm by myself. I'm afraid of a home invasion which happened to the Franks, their door left unlocked not as an invitation to strangers, just until the moving van came, but they were robbed though left unharmed, the telephone wires cut, and warned to wait half an hour before alerting anyone.

I went up to the second floor to look in the Franklin Busybody, an arrangement of mirrors said to be invented by Benjamin Franklin. Lee has attached it to one of the front windows of the living room. By maneuvering your gaze, you should be able to see who is below at the door, at least, that is its purpose. But this time I couldn't, only made out the wet doorstep. I imagined who it could have been and created scenarios of why; for instance, it might have been Cara across the street who had locked herself out walking Prince (for Prince Charming), a shelter dog she got when she was looking for a cat, and he must have seemed to her like a starved, shaved cat when she found him, shivering and rubbing up against her leg because it was winter. A pronounced under bite made him even more pathetic, but now his fur has grown in, he might even be part Schnauzer, and he's a handsome, red-haired little guy, with a bushy mustache over his mouth you have to push back to see the misaligned teeth. He is so good-looking, in fact, Cara wants to send him to school for training as a therapy dog, so she can take him to retirement communities to delight old people. She thinks these days too many dogs are brought only to kindergartens for little children to play with.

And I worried she had forgotten her key on one of the many walks Prince requires, which is his one remaining flaw. This was a possibility and I'd have felt quite bad not to open the door to her. So I invented another narrative of who was knocking and why, that it might be the scraggly blond guy with a petition to put his candidate, maybe his brother-in-law, on the ballot for mayor, which already had six unknowns running; he seemed to show up in the rain and at night, I thought, to encourage sympathy for his cause. I answered, unaccountably once, I saw him in the busybody, which reminds me a little of a stereopticon when you get it right, there are so many angles of sight, but I discouraged him, saying I couldn't chat just then, that I was busy. Or it might even have been a delivery person though we weren't expecting anything, but you never know.

What the Little Girl Across the Street
Will Remember

THAT SHE ASKED HER MOTHER IF THEY COULD PLAY BALL EARLY in the morning. That her mother said, "I have to go to work," and after a little thought, "O.K., hurry and get your ball." That she came out with it and they played, the mother running in the street in front of the house as often as the girl did after the pink rubber ball when it escaped her or grazed her mother's fuchsia-painted nails.

That her father let her sit on his lap, stroking her hair, till she was nearly fifteen.

That there was a swimming pool in the basement they came home to and all swam and played in with a beach ball before supper.

That every birthday, a party was held in her honor with balloons and streamers out the door so the other children would know where to come with their presents, electronic games, stickers and coloring books, Barbie dolls. That they all petted her adoring and well-behaved Portuguese Water Dog, Woofie. And that much later, when the parties ceased, there would still be a white birthday cake with her name on it in pink and blue icing she could count on finding on the kitchen table when all of her other, outside fun was exhausted.

That when she closed the door for the last time ever, she would leave a profound silence that the house would never recover from.

In Back of Us

I am three, flat in the long grass.
The sun hovers, wavers on its gladiolus stem,
my belly pressed to the small yellow fires
of dandelions, buttercups,
over me, dense
the bodies of insects heating up.

I hear my mother call my name.
It wriggles toward me
like a thin black snake.

THERE WAS A BACKYARD BEHIND US ONLY FOR THOSE FIRST FOUR years of my life when we lived in Logan. Now perhaps no houses remain, only a low meadow; I am told the houses have sunk into the ground in terminal moraine.

No one cut the grass in our backyard. A wood and wire fence staggered along three sides where my mother planted purple morning glories that mounted the posts. You could get lost in that yard, especially if you were little. It cut you off from anywhere. We rented the house and didn't speak to the neighbors. There had been a fire and half the back of the house was missing. I remember a wooden swing on a frame that I sat in with my mother and sometimes Sidney, but he didn't like to swing with me because my legs were too short and he had to do all the work. I suppose the grown-ups went out to it on sweltering evenings. It kicked up a little breeze and gave you a scent of grass and flowers. I scratched and scratched bites of mosquitoes who found me in that yard.

Turned Away

AND SOMETIME DURING THOSE FIRST FOUR YEARS I REMEMBER MY father turning away from me, the shine in his eyes dulling when he looked at me. It was like the window shade coming down. Was that why I gave myself over to Leo, to take his place?

Did I remind my father of her, my mother? They didn't seem to like each other often then. But no, he said I looked like the lost mother he had so loved. When was it exactly that I became to my father a burden, not his joy, only one more person in the crowded house with the back burnt away? Another person waiting for the bathroom. Someone else he had to earn money to provide for.

Order decreases as we go forward, Stephen Hawking said. That is, the present is ever-deteriorating, crumbling into an expanding universe. So I do not only imagine the order of the past. Family, like Atlantis, a continent that cannot be recovered but just resurfaces in the fragments of memory. I remember, then, my father's thick, square workman's hands with the rounded, ridged, domelike nails. Is he holding my small hand in his?

I cover the past with a drop cloth to keep the present from spilling over.

A Letter

WALKING INTO THE TOO QUIET, TOO EMPTY HOUSE, I FEEL MY FA-
ther's presence. The chair where he sat a little separate from the
rest of us, the green mohair armchair under the lamp, to read the
Bulletin after work. A familiar stranger. So rare when he looked
up to smile, to speak, I couldn't remember if he actually had or if
it was something I'd only wished for. But how important just his
presence, how glad I was we could count on it, even if we knew
to leave him alone.

I look up at the polished hardwood stairs where he once
caught me when I stumbled down from the second floor. "Dol-
ly!" he cried out. He came running and cradled my head in his
arms, closer maybe than we'd ever been. And in a loving, gentle
voice as he held me, he crooned, "Dolly, are you all right? You're
all right?" So I saw him, on the stairs too, kneeling over me.
And at the kitchen table, in a desperate hunger that must have
haunted him from childhood, stuffing in mouthfuls he scarcely
looked at.

In the years they lived alone together, after the rest of us were
gone, did my mother stand over him, serving, or join him with
her plate at the side of the table? I can see them sitting together,
talking quietly (could they?) as they ate. I hoped that was how it
was. And imagined them, evenings, watching the TV in silence,
keeping each other company. I knew there were middle-of-the-
night calls to the hospital when the paramedics came, another
heart attack or the fear of one. But easy sleep too, maybe, other
nights. Or did they stay up arguing, gnashing over my father's
concerns, as they had done all those nights I couldn't sleep,
hearing them from my bed in the middle room? And were the

enemies that had mocked and threatened him all now locked within his body and taking the shape of illnesses?

For a while after he retired, he had fitted up a cutting bench and a wheel to work on diamonds at home. He would, of course, want to help Leo, who had taken over the shop downtown. A space was swept and cleared out in the dark jumble of the cellar and a standing lamp brought down. I could see him, smiling to himself, the jeweler's loupe to his eye, dimples in his cheeks like Sidney's. Maybe Leo didn't need him but Daddy would want to believe he did, that he could still keep his hand in, be useful.

There was a tender pride he took in me too at the end of his life which was new. Instead of discouraging my ambition to be a writer—as he had when I was in school, "Only one in a million makes it"—he hoped I'd put my maiden name, his name, on the masthead of the union newspaper I edited. But it was too late; I'd already started with my married name. Oh, I wished I'd changed it just to please him.

Unthinkable, that I would never now be able to sit with him, his arm thrown over my shoulder, as I'd wished for and imagined a million times.

To reach my mother in the kitchen I must first pass through the dining room. Odd designation because it was so rarely used for dining, only on holidays or the two times my brothers invite the women they will marry to our house to meet the family. Not true, sometimes even after the marriage, on occasional Friday nights for Shabbos dinner. Leo's wife Bobbi will hate these evenings, the same plain food, a stuffed capon, oven-roasted potatoes, an overdone vegetable, but fresh, not canned. She'll be dressed up with earrings and perfume for their date afterward, a movie or a party. For reserved, red-haired Selma, in awe of Sidney's mother, this dinner is an evening out. I appreciate the variety and company, my mother's efforts at preparation despite her advanced years when most dinners are leftover-based. I try to be at home those evenings, glad the room and the house don't recede into their usual darkness.

If we had something like an altar to household gods, it would be positioned here in the dining room. It's an odd room with a conglomeration of furniture, Louis XIV to Scandinavian modern and everything in between. The large wooden dining table, ladder chairs with crisscrossed panels pulled under it, that my mother stood before to light candles on Friday nights. The same table I did stunts and roller-skated on when I was a child. Lining the walls are a china closet, a buffet, and a bureau with a mirror above it, remnants of previous households, my family's or second-hand purchases from a neighbor who was moving. An embroidered scarf is spread over the bureau and what surprises and touches me, it's topped with my framed high school graduation picture. I think of my mother's face behind me once in the mirror watching me comb my hair. Out of nowhere she said, wistfully, fondly, "You have a noble forehead, like your father."

And I remember her fresh from the shower, hair just washed in Emulsified Coconut Oil Shampoo. The sweet smell moves with her, even after she ties her toweled hair in a flowered silk kerchief. It wafts with her down the stairs to the dining room where she has already laid out silver candlesticks on one side of the white, lace-edged tablecloth in preparation. She takes up a book of matches that came with Sidney's cigarettes and strikes one that she sets to the wicks of both candles. There is no other light in the dusky room. Then she closes her eyes, praying, and waves her arms in wide arcs. The shadows of her movements beat against the walls like wings of a great, dark bird.

Other articles of faith were stored in the top drawer of the mirrored bureau, red and blue velvet drawstring pouches where the *tefillin* were kept that my brothers wrapped around their arms to say daily morning prayers, nodding their heads forward and back, and my father did, too, once in a while. They could have seen themselves in the mirror above as they *davened* but didn't look. I have a flash in my mind even now of one of them with the square leather phylactery on his forehead, looking like an Egyptian god. Also kept here, yarmulkes and prayer books in Hebrew I couldn't read. That's where the holiness ended. Embossed tablecloths and napkins and fill-in linens from the dime store were laid in the drawers below.

It's late afternoon. I've been with my mother a few days now. The dining room is partially lit by a thread of sun from the one window at the side and rear where my family's house divides from the neighbor's. My mother comes out from the kitchen which is and always has been her habitual lair and into the dining room to sit with me, as if I were a guest. She's remembered I don't belong here.

"What will you do with his things?" I ask. I'm thinking I could help her pack them up.

"Sidney is coming for the shirts and jackets and his bathrobe. Not the underwear."

"What for?"

She raises her eyebrows, looks at me like I'm an idiot. "He'll wear them. But not the underwear. It's too big."

At first I think this is in the interest of thrift, a little creepy. But then I understand. He wants to put on clothes my father wore, as if to find something of him still inside.

And when my mother leaves the room, when she in fact goes up the stairs for the bathroom or to rest, I'm drawn to the hall closet where my father's overcoat and hats were kept, and the cardigan he wore around the house. It's not my house any longer, hasn't been for years. I feel like I'm trespassing, but some force draws me to the pearl knob and, after a moment's hesitation, I turn it and pull the door open. The gray hat and the brown hat share the upper shelf, just as he'd have left them. Wearing a hat inside was bad luck, a superstition of my mother's. But my father wore one to *daven* in, it was what old men tended to wear even in synagogue. I reach for the worn felt brim of the closer one and take it down. My fingers circle the indentation, the crease my father pinched into the crown every time he wore it. It's soft and cool. I could be holding my hand over his hand as it makes the familiar motion.

When my mother returns, she tells me she doesn't want to forget, she has something for me. She goes to the bureau, opens the religious drawer. I've walked over with her and see that the prayer books remain, though both brothers have taken the velvet pouches to their new homes. But something else is inside as well. She hands me a letter in a cancelled envelope with Italian words stamped over it and in English, "Return to Sender."

"It came back," she says. I recognize my father's gaping handwriting, the wrong spelling for the street of my Roman address. I can't breathe. I sit down, staring at the envelope. The letter hasn't been opened, she hasn't read it. It's a talisman to her too, I decide. I can't seem to lift out the folded pages, they might be bars of lead. Does she recognize how important this is?

What must my father have thought not to get a response? When I left for Europe, I promised I'd write. And I did. Several times. I told him about the scary, exciting drive through the Alps, the fast roads and overhangs, how warm Rome was when we got there, how beautiful and green, the hilly streets and unexpected palm trees. About the new apartment where the light, provisional furniture seemed to be dancing, the terrace edged with cactuses and how often in the evening you could sit and watch the sky fill up with fireworks for the many saints' days. So much that I'd wanted to share. But not getting an answer, I thought my father had moved back to my mother's stance of anger at me and disapproval.

I could remember the warmth that blossomed between us though when, after I eloped with, yes, Phil, he confided, "I heard of a couple who couldn't get married and they killed themselves." Was he thinking of Romeo and Juliet? But he gave me his blessing, admitting that the important thing to him was that I be happy.

So painful it was then, leaving him when I feared for his health, when I visited daily as he lay in his hospital bed. After he recovered and went home, I asked the cardiologist and of course he wouldn't say I shouldn't go, that my father's life was in danger. In other families, children went away all the time, to colleges or other cities. Just not in mine, especially since I was a girl. I had never left as had so many friends. I lived even after my marriage for several years in the same city, my brothers, in fact, had done so their whole lives. But all that time my young husband and I both were like horses at the gate, panting to take off. We wanted to see the world that childhood, a lack of money, and our families held us back from. We dreamed of living in a foreign country, ex-pats, famous authors, wanting never to come back. And after a couple of years of working and saving, we left Philadelphia for the first time.

How could I doubt my father's love? Yet I was hurt when no answer came to my letters. Was it guilt, shame, more likely the self-doubt that had been fostered all my life? Anyhow, out of despair or a will to toughen myself against disappointment, I stopped writing to him. I sent letter after letter to my brother Leo, though, almost a diary of my new life. And Leo answered in his beautiful, florid hand. I thought he would share the letters with the rest of the family, but possibly he hadn't, out of regard for my father's feelings, thinking he'd be hurt the letters weren't coming to him. All my father really wanted to know, I was sure, was that

I was well and hadn't been sold into white slavery—how many times had I laughed about that notion of his? But also, I knew in my heart he'd want proof of the continuing bond between us. I hoped Leo would at least have reassured him that everything was O.K. But if he hadn't?

Daddy's letter. Touching, sad, in retrospect. I'd told him we landed in London and he talked about the buying trip he'd once taken there. I was full of details, the first time I had seen anyone ski, a visit to the Colosseum, other trivia that at the time had seemed momentous. His was a kind and loving letter. He wished us well and begged me to come back soon to visit. I knew it wasn't easy for him to offer up his feelings like this. Oh, if only the letter had come when it was meant to, if I had been able to read it then, the difference it would have made.

ELAINE TERRANOVA is the author of nine collections of poems, most recently, *Perdido*, released also as an audio book. An earlier book, *Dollhouse*, was winner of the Off the Grid Press 2013 Poetry Award. She received the 1990 Walt Whitman Award from the Academy of American Poets for her first book, *The Cult of the Right Hand*. Her translation of Euripides' *Iphigenia at Aulis* was published in the Penn Greek Drama Series. Her work was part of the Poetry Society's Poetry in Motion project. Among her awards are a Pushcart Prize, a Pew Fellowship in the Arts, the Banister residency at Sweet Briar College, the Judah Magnus Award, two Pennsylvania Council on the Arts fellowships, and a National Endowment in the Arts Fellowship in Literature. Her poetry has appeared in *The New Yorker*, *The American Poetry Review*, *Ploughshares*, and other magazines and anthologies.

For many years she was an instructor in English and Creative Writing in the Philadelphia area at the Community College of Philadelphia, Temple University, the University of Delaware, Curtis Institute, and in the Rutgers, Camden MFA Program. She also worked as a manuscript editor at J.B. Lippincott and as a free-lance writer and editor.

CPSIA information can be obtained
at www.ICGtesting.com
Printed in the USA
BVHW070819170321
602755BV00001B/136